Dispatches from Our Corner of the Globe

Dispatches from Our Corner of the Globe

Lew Hudson

*To Bill and Helen
Thanks for your friendship
Lew Hudson*

Compiled & Edited by
Rebecca Hudson

Copyright © 2012 Rebecca Hudson
All rights reserved.
ISBN: 1466494484
ISBN-13: 978-1-466-49448-0

The material in this book originally appeared in the Worthington Daily Globe and Brainerd Daily Dispatch newspapers and are reprinted with permission.

Library of Congress Cataloging-in-Publication Data

Hudson, Lew
  Dispatches from our corner of the globe/by Lew Hudson : compiled and edited by Rebecca Hudson. — 1st ed.
ISBN 978-1-466-49448-0   ISBN-13 1-466-49448-4 (pbk.)
1. Minnesota—Social Life & Customs. 2. Essays—Miscellanea. 3. Minnesota—Humor. 4. Family Life—Humor. 5. Marriage and Family Life. I. Hudson, Rebecca. II. Title. 2012
808.84 dc22

DEDICATION

My dear family, it is with all my love that
I dedicate this book to you.
I treasure you all.

~Sisters LuAnn and Cindy who, even though
they consider the day that I learned to operate
a doorknob the darkest one of their lives
and were a perpetual source of hand-me-down clothes,
we still manage to be the best of friends.
~Brother Fred, whose sheer delight in tormenting his older
sisters, especially me, has always made life interesting.
~My sons, Christopher and Patrick, for your unconditional love that
makes being a mother so very worthwhile.
~And of course our wonderful Mother and Father.

CONTENTS

1 Never a Dull Moment   1
2 Family Reflections   61
3 Hudson's Theorem   109
4 A Sporting Chance   159
5 Holiday Follies   181
6 Politics As Usual   195
7 Music Hath Charms...   221
8 Technicalities   245
9 Uninvited Guests   273

Chapter 1

Never a Dull Moment

Dad and "Mrs. H", as he affectionately referred to her in his columns, have enjoyed many rewarding years of marriage together, more than 60 to be exact. Throughout that time, Dad dutifully and honorably provided for mom, three daughters, and one son. Ours was a humble yet very loving upbringing and we all share endearing recollections of childhood. It is safe to say that dad may have retained his own sanity by periodically slipping into a reverie of contemplation. He has always been a great philosopher and has given importance to even the slightest, most mundane mysteries of life. Gradually, Mom and Dad learned to adapt as one after another of their kids left the nest. They have for many years now been best friends and companions. But having Dad around the house, Mom would attest, means there certainly has never been a dull moment.

Lew Hudson

Creature of Habit

Do you ever get out of sync? It happened to me the other day when I dropped the soap while showering. It slid around the tub a time or two and skidded to a stop. At least it sounded like it did. My eyes were full of soap so I couldn't see.

I rinsed my face, turned around, located the bar and picked it up. But then I couldn't remember where I'd left off in the scrubbing process. So I had to start all over. That ruined my morning.

It put me behind schedule, which meant I had to hurry getting dressed, which made me forget my hat when I went out the door, which meant the sun was in my eyes while I was driving to work, which meant my head started to ache, which meant I had to stop and buy a tin of aspirin, which not only made me late for work but also ruined my usually placid disposition.

I'm a creature of habit. Anything that disrupts my regimen throws me for a loop. I remember a psychologist in college explaining why human beings develop rituals. In times of severe emotional stress, when everything in life is crumbling, he said, a ritual gives folks something solid to cling to.

In everyday terms, he said, people value rituals because they can follow them unconsciously. That's for me. In the morning I'm incapable of conscious thought. Ritual sustains me through that first hour.

Take breakfast, for example. It's been a glass of orange juice, a cup of coffee, a bowl of Wheaties and a slice of toast with grape jam for as long as I can remember. Mrs. H, who isn't quite as ritual-bound, can't understand this. For years she's been searching unsuccessfully for a cereal worthy of her loyalty.

Because she keeps changing, she thinks I should too. "Don't you ever get tired of Wheaties and grape jam?" she asks. How can I get tired of something I'm not aware I'm eating? If she'd put a bowl of corn flakes in front of me I'd be lost.

First, I'd have to decide whether I like cornflakes. Worse yet, from that point on I'd have to decide every day which cereal I wanted. I couldn't take that. Can you imagine life among variety pack families, faced with 10 cereal choices? That would be worse than death. No, I'm a Wheaties and grape jam man. Always have been. Always will be. It's simpler that way. I just plod down that comfortable rut as content as can be. Leave the surprises for birthdays.

In Search of a No Fault Lifestyle

"Why is it," I asked, "that it is always my fault when something bad happens?" Mrs. H and I had been out to dinner and were on the way from the Holiday Inn the other evening. She was driving.

As we approached Sixth and Quince she pulled over into the new center turning lane. We were talking. I said It looks like people are getting used to the turn lanes since there don't seem to be as many close calls as when the restriping was done last month.

At that point, the light went yellow and Mrs. H slammed on the brakes. "I almost went ahead and turned," she said. "You were talking."

What my talking had to do with her turning, I don't know. But suddenly I became aware that, by some strange quirk of logic, had she run that light it would have been my fault.

It happens that way more often than not. A mosquito bit her on the arm the other evening. "You must have let it in from the garage," she said. Maybe I did. Maybe I didn't. I was out there a short time before, but who knows? It could just as well have come in with her when she came home from work. That thought never occurred to her.

About that time a car sped through the intersection. "See

that?" I asked. "If you had gone on through that guy would have hit you broadside and the policeman in the car behind us would have been a witness."

Actually, there wasn't a police car in sight but I thought I'd shake her up a little. She doesn't shake easily. Instead she reminded me that while I have had three speeding convictions and three accidents in the last 40 years her driving record is squeaky clean.

"Not squeaky clean," I said. "Don't you remember that time in 1951 when you misjudged things a little and scraped the retaining wall outside our basement garage?"

She flinched a little. She always does when I bring that up. It happened shortly after she had obtained her driver's license and was still a little tentative about operating a car. To her credit, it's the first, last and only time she has ever put a mark on a car, but it's something she'd like to forget.

She thought a moment or two. The light changed. She turned the corner. We headed down the street. And then she said, just loud enough for me to hear, "I've never had a ticket but if I ever do, I've decided it will be your fault."

A Puzzling Tale

Mrs. H loves crossword puzzles, quiz shows and riddles. To hear her tell it, solving me has been her toughest to date.

Every week we go through the same routine. She buys her favorite magazine and turns immediately to the crossword puzzle. First she checks last week's answers to see if she missed any. Then she starts on the new one. I usually don't hear much out of her for a half hour or so as she fills in the obvious blanks.

By this time she knows all the odd-ball words the puzzle writers use…aba (a three-letter word for fabric woven from the hair of camels or goats), wynd (a four-letter word for a very narrow street), yana (a four-letter word for a Russian river flowing into the Laptev Sea), or Laptev (a six-letter word for a sea into which the Yana River flows).

But after a while she slows down. Pretty soon there's less writing and more dictionary consulting, fewer smiles and more frowns, less illumination and more frustration. Eventually all progress grinds to a halt.

That's when I try to be helpful. After all, isn't that a husband's duty?

It happened the other evening. Just before she stalled

completely, I casually volunteered my services. "Let me see if I can help," I said cheerily.

She didn't even look up. "I am a writer," I said. "I make my living with words." One eye turned up and gave me a fishy stare. "Hey," I said, "maybe there's one subject I know something about."

"Not likely," she said.

"Men do know some things women don't customarily pay much attention to," I countered.

"Name one," she said. My memory failed me about that time.

"Just give me a try," I ventured. "I want to play too."

"I did once and you made up a word," she said. She's got a memory like an elephant.

"That's true," I replied, "but you have to admit it fit the space and sounded reasonable."

"Humph," she said.

That took care of the matter until almost time for the 10 p.m. news when I tried again. "Did I ever tell you spelling was one of my stronger subjects in school," I said.

"OK," she said. "Try this one. What's a four-letter word for a children's dance step?"

That really hurt. My blabber-mouthed aunt, who was my second-grade teacher before she married my uncle, made the mistake once of telling Mrs. H about the darkest school day of my entire life...the day everyone found out I couldn't skip. It was "fizz-ed" time and Miss Smith, as she was then known, had the entire class playing a sort of skip around the circle game. I don't remember the purpose of it all but I do remember what it did to my social standing at North English Grade School.

I couldn't skip. Try as I could I couldn't get my feet to shuffle in any sort of orderly fashion. All I could muster was an ungainly, wobbling walk. I was the only kid in school...probably the only kid in the entire universe who didn't know how to skip. No one could possibly have been so dumb as to be unable to get the hang of skipping...but I was.

To this day I still twinge at the memory. Tears filled my eyes. I wanted to crawl into the inkwell on my desk and drown myself. It took at least until the second semester of fifth grade before the kids quit teasing me.

"That word is 'skip'," I said, "but it's not really in that puzzle you're working is it?"

"That's right," she said. "And neither are you."

Lew Hudson

Ever Feel Like You May Be a Winner?

"What's the number going to be?" I asked her. We had finished supper and were drinking coffee. On the TV they were getting ready to draw the Daily Three lottery numbers.

"470," said Mrs. H.

"OK," I said, "let's see."

The first ball up was a four. The second was a seven. The third was a zero. It was uncanny. "How'd you know that?" I asked

"Oh, just a feeling," she said. Unfortunately a feeling was all she had. She hadn't bought a ticket.

"Next time you get a feeling," I said, "let me know ahead of time and we'll make it worthwhile." She promised she would. Feelings, though, can't be turned on or off like faucets. Since then, she has been absolutely numb.

The experience got me wondering if I've been underestimating this wife of mine. If she's starting to feel lottery vibes, I'm going to start paying serious attention.

Back in the days when we had a house full of kids and a shoebox full of bills, she signed up for a drawing at the supermarket. Top prize was half a hog. When they called to tell her she had won, she celebrated. I didn't. It cost me $75 for a used freezer to store it.

Another time she signed up at an anniversary celebration at a restaurant. Top prize was a silver coffee service. She won it. That time all I had to buy was the polish to keep it shiny.

Another time she won a gift certificate at a style show. The store that offered it, however, was 75 miles up the road and it cost me a tank of gas to drive up there to collect.

Me, I'm a stranger to winning. As far as I can remember, I've won only twice. Once was at a spring style show. The sponsor had lined up a bushel of door prizes---merchandise certificates, clothing, dinners at local restaurants and a grand-prize vacation weekend.

Toward the end, they held up a six-inch plastic Statue of Liberty bank and started fishing for a ticket. "I'm getting a feeling," Mrs. H said, "but I sure hope I'm wrong. I don't know what I'd do if I won an ugly thing like that."

She didn't. I did. The other time? That was about 41 years ago. I won her.

Mr. H Doesn't Bother Reaching Out

I don't very often answer the phone around our house. Force of habit, I guess. Other than when Brother David the Iowan has called to harangue me with accounts of how well the Hawkeyes were doing, or Brother Bob the other Iowan has called to con me into taking him fishing, I can remember only a handful of times in the last 25 years when a phone call was for me.

It started about the time the kids got into junior high and has continued to the present day, even though Mrs. H and I are the only ones living at our house now.

Son Fred came home on a weekend holiday from college a month or so ago. Precisely 43 seconds after he walked in the front door the phone rang. Mrs. H reached for it. "Don't bother," I said. "It's for Fred." It was.

"How do they know," she asked?

"Search me," I said.

Our daughters, when they're home visiting accuse me of being deaf. "Don't you hear the phone ring, Dad?" I hear it. It's just that I don't do anything about it.

Mrs. H is my telephone answerer. She's also my letter writer, scheduler and organizer. That's something we worked out many years ago. "Why else," I said, "would a man with matrimony on his mind seek out a professional secretary?"

That always makes her feel good. A woman appreciates being needed. Besides, she enjoys talking on the phone. We try to call our three daughters and one son about once a week. She gets on the main phone and talks and I get on the extension and listen. Every once in a while I crowd a word in edgeways.

Other than that, when the phone rings I just keep on reading the paper. Unlike the English poet John Dunne, I don't tend to ask for whom the bell tolls. It never tolls for me.

But Mrs. H gets into some of the most delightful conversations. The other day, the phone rang and someone said, "Grandma?" Mrs. H said, "I'm a grandma, all right but I don't think I'm yours." After a brief pause the line went dead.

"She sounded like such a nice little girl," Mrs. H said. "I would have enjoyed talking to her."

Mrs. H views wrong number calls as opportunities to make new friends. She's had some of the nicest conversations with people she didn't know and won't ever talk to again. She's even been known to converse with those computerized voices that call every once in a while to sell time-share condos or announce that an order has arrived.

It happened not long ago. "I felt like the village idiot," she said. "This mechanical computer voice told me my order was in and I said, 'Thank you.' There was another one more recently. The phone rang. She picked it up and a voice said, "This is a recording. All our operators are busy. Will you wait a moment?" She said, "OK". Soft music filled her ear for a few moments. Then a live voice came on, but instead of telling her whatever it was they were selling, said, "I have a recorded message I want you to hear." That was a bit more than even she could stand. The telephone cord curled a little tighter as she expressed her opinion on that approach to electronic sales.

"What really makes me mad," she said, "are wrong number callers who hang up without saying a word or, even worse, try and blame me for the fact that they got a wrong number."

Mrs. H is the sort of person who just can't stand to hear a telephone ring. She's been known to run all the way from the far corner of the lot, stumble up the steps, dash in the house, grab the phone and breathlessly say, "Hello".

Me, I blissfully ignore it. If it rings while I'm out in the garage or down in the basement, my conscience doesn't bother me in the least to just let it ring. In the first place, it won't be for me and in the second, there is Bell's Law, which proclaims, "The last ring will occur as you pick up the receiver."

If it's important they'll call back. If it isn't, who cares?

Lew Hudson

Reporter Learns a Costly Lesson

We're back.

To say Mrs. H and I were happy to return to work Monday is to understate the obvious. She is walking on the new hip joint she received June 4, and I'm getting used to my mended heart. We are wiser. We have learned how swiftly life can change.

My lesson came at 2:15 a.m., June 25 – the hour my heart almost quit. Did it come as a surprise? Not exactly. Every male in my family for three generations has experienced heart trouble by their early 60's. Hoping to become an exception, I kept in good shape. If my destination was within a mile, I walked. I chose the stairs rather than the elevator. I gave up smoking 23 years ago. My weight was normal. My cholesterol count was 167.

But my genes were still Hudson's, and the time bomb was ticking. When the danger signals came—brief incidents of pressure and pain in the center of my chest—I knew what they meant. But I rationalized. It was not, I told myself, a convenient time for heart trouble.

Seven times I was warned—four times the afternoon and evening before my attack. But I did nothing. I said nothing. That stubborn stupidity almost cost me my life. When I awoke at 2:15 a.m., there was no more rationalizing. A heart attack gets your undivided attention.

A call to 911 brought help in a hurry. A deputy sheriff arrived in about two minutes. A North Ambulance crew was only a minute or two behind. Together they brought me back from the edge on which I was teetering.

Hundreds of times on the police scanner I have heard incoming ambulance crews radio a patient's vital signs to the hospital. This time, as we raced down Washington Street, it was mine they were giving. They weren't good.

The emergency room nurse met the ambulance before it stopped. I was rushed inside. I don't remember everything that happened after that, but I do remember that every time I awoke, a doctor or nurse was at my side.

As soon as I was up to it, they transferred me to the St. Cloud Hospital for an angiogram to determine the extent of damage and what best to do about it. It is a fascinating procedure. A probe is inserted in the artery and threaded to the heart, where dye is released into the blood vessels. On the monitor I watched my own heart as the doctors pointed out blockages that were threatening my life.

There were four. A clear case for coronary bypass surgery. It is scary business. In a five hour operation the chest is split open and the heart stopped so the surgeon can perform the delicate procedure. Veins are taken from the leg and stitched into place to bypass the clogged arteries.

Few operations are more traumatic. My brother Hawkeye Bob, who had five bypasses three years ago, said it was like being hit by a semi-trailer truck. Bob exaggerates. It's more like being flattened by a Greyhound bus.

Despite the trauma, the fatality rate is low—about 4 percent among patients who have suffered heart attacks and about 2 percent otherwise. Recovery is remarkably rapid. Although I didn't think much of the idea, two nurses had me walking within 48 hours. The third day two nurses had me walking by myself. The fifth day I went a mile in several excursions up and down the corridor. The seventh day I came home.

And now both of us are back at work. For the first time in years, Mrs. H is walking without pain. For the first time in eight weeks I'm concentrating on something other than a sore chest. Our experiences have made us acutely aware of the healing power that flows from the concern of family and friends.

Between us we received more than 250 cards and more prayers than we will ever know. We are deeply thankful. And every day is a glorious experience to be savored.

Lew Hudson

Tune in to New Sound: Conversation

I feel sorry for young people with all that powerful stereo equipment in their cars. A fellow pulled up beside me at a stoplight last week. His windows were down and the intersection echoed with what sounded like a highly amplified cat fight going on in his car.

My ears hurt. I can't imagine what it was like over there. Obviously if he isn't deaf yet he surely will be before he's 25. And then he'll miss out on one of life's more rewarding experiences—conversations in the car.

Travel for Mrs. H and me is an occasion for talking without interruption. We were on the road a week or so ago. For about 300 miles we didn't even turn on the radio. We talked. After all these years you'd think we would have explored about every subject, told every joke and related every experience in our lives, but such is not the case. We're still learning about each other.

She was telling about growing up on the farm down in Iowa. She told me how they'd pick up a chicken, tuck its head under its wing and rock it back and forth a few times. It seems to hypnotize the dim-witted creatures. Set them down, she said, and they'd stand there like statues for several minutes.

She talked about the time her parents were away for the day and her older brother was looking after things. It was a steaming August day. He was trying to get some hogs to go where he wanted rather than where they wanted. As usual, the hogs were winning. In frustration he picked up a hammer and hurled it, striking one squarely between the eyes and killing it instantly.

That is not a wise thing to do on a non-electrified Iowa farm in August. Butchering is nasty enough in the chill of November. In the heat of summer, it is just plain disgusting.

Why memories most often revolve around summer days, we wondered. Didn't anything ever happen in winter?

And then she was off with another yarn about the time she and her sisters were holding a funeral for a dead chicken. They were just getting to the interesting part when a car pulled in. It was Mrs. Snell, the piano teacher. Mrs. Snell, she said, was a large woman who wore those silky dresses favored by rural women in the 1930's. Summers, the only season when there was time for piano lessons, were always hot. Deodorant had not yet been invented. Mrs. Snell smelled.

"And that's why I never learned to play the piano," she said matter-of-factly.

Fishing? She said she learned to fish long before she ever caught anything. "How'd you do that?" I asked innocently. "I'd take the dog and go down to the road ditch out of sight of the house and pretend-fish with a stick and a length of string."

"No hook?" I asked. "Nope."

To ease her conscience, she said, she always went just far enough from the house so she couldn't honestly determine whether they were calling her or someone else to help with the dishes.

"Vacation Bible School," she continued. "I hated it." The only one in the neighborhood was about five miles away in a Friend's church. "We didn't know anybody there and didn't want to go—I cried about half the time."

"They used to make us answer roll call with a Bible verse. 'Jesus Wept'—that's the shortest one in the Bible—but someone always grabbed it before it got to me, and then I'd have to say I couldn't think of any and all the kids would laugh." To this day, she maintains the name of that church was a misnomer.

"I was in high school when we got electricity," she said. While it was great, the wiring left something to be desired. Her grandfather owned their farm and a half-dozen others. Obviously he didn't get them by spending money unnecessarily. His idea of electric lighting, she said, was a bare bulb hanging from a cord in the center of each room.

The separator, though, still had to be cranked by hand and its dozens of discs individually washed and dried.

And so it went—story after story as the miles rolled by. Nothing very important in the scheme of history—just homey experiences to which people can relate, experiences that collectively make people what they are.

Like turning a soiled dress inside out when it was the only one she had and she needed to present a fresh appearance to the world—of riding to town in the back of the pickup truck because there was no family car—of Sunday School offerings tied in the corner of a handkerchief for safe keeping—of cutting paper dolls from the pages of mail order catalogs—these and other stories rolled out in a nostalgic procession.

Conversations in the car—one of our favorite pastimes. I feel sorry for that young man with the loud stereo. I doubt he'll ever discover how much fun it can be.

Lew Hudson

The Games We Play

Somehow or other I don't think the guy who wrote that song about the games people play had us in mind. We're checkers and rummy people. That is, we used to be. Nowadays we play cribbage. It's better that way.

Rummy is her game. Checkers is mine. Cribbage is neutral ground. We found that out early in our marriage. One rainy Sunday afternoon before we had even thought about a TV set or the patter of little feet, we sat down to play checkers. It started amiably enough, but after four or five moves things got a little intense.

I saw an opportunity. "If I move this one and she lets me get away with it," I thought, "I'll have her where I want her. I'll be able to trade one checker for three of hers." I moved. She didn't respond. I baited my trap. "You have a jump," I said.

"No I don't," she replied.

"You have to jump," I said. "It's in the book."

"Not in mine," she said.

"The rule is that you have to jump," I demanded.

"If you're going to make up the rules as we go along," she said, "I just won't play." We never did finish that game. Instead we played rummy. Now rummy is a simple game. It's a game that draws as much on luck of the draw as it does on skill of the players.

At least that's what I had always thought before we were married. Now I'm not so sure. In 41 years of marriage I have yet to win a Rummy game from Mrs. H. How can you explain 500 consecutive losses in a game of chance? I've tried everything. Sometimes I play to get all my cards down on the table quickly and catch her with a bunch of count. She counters by picking up everything in sight. Even when I get my cards down first she has enough to bury me.

Other times I try her tactic—picking up the discards and trying for high points. That's when she calmly lays down her hand leaving me with a fistful of garbage.

I've tried different ways of shuffling and cutting the deck, walking around the table, diversionary tactics, small talk, soft soap, threats—you name it, I've tried it. The result is always the same. She wins.

No one can be that lucky. Luck evens itself out over time. No dry spell ever lasts 41 years. So, it must be skill. Somewhere in her dim dark past she must have learned how to stack a deck. That's got to be it.

Try as I may, though, I can't catch her at it. She's too good for me. The only way I'll ever redeem myself is to get her into a checker game. But do you think she'll play?

"Not unless you're willing to play by the rules," she says.

Eating Apple Pie Leads to Problems

"What", she said, "are you doing?" Over the years I've become accustomed to that question. It's one I've answered dozens of times as I've tried to explain my idiosyncrasies to the woman with whom I have shared my life for almost 40 years.

This time, I was eating a piece of apple pie. "What do you mean?" I asked innocently.

"That pie," she said. "Why are you eating it that way?"

Now I've been eating apple pie since I was a child and, except when I've been at a picnic or in a hurry, I've used a fork.

"I'm eating a piece of pie with a fork," I said.

"Not that," she said. "The way you're eating it. Why are you starting on the crust end?"

"Because that's the way pie should be eaten," I replied. "It's the only way."

She snorted in disbelief. "I've watched you eat pie a thousand times," she said, "and I've never seen you eat it that way."

"Then you just haven't been looking," I replied. "I nip the tip off first and then turn it sideways and start on the crust. Haven't you noticed how I do it?"

"Normal people," she said, "start at the tip end and leave the crust until last."

"That's the trouble with being normal," I countered. "You end up with a dry piece of crust with no goodies."

"Besides," I said, "I follow the save-the-best-for-last theory. When you eat pie my way, the last piece is the one just behind the tip. That's the part of the pie that gets the most sugar."

"What's more, "I continued, "if the pie happens to be over-baked, the crust is dark and crispy. If it's under-baked, the center is soggy. But either way the piece behind the tip is always just right."

She shook her head. "You've done that all your life?" she asked incredulously.

"The only way to go," I said.

She fell silent. That doesn't happen often.

I knew what she was thinking. Communication without conversation is a byproduct of a long marriage.

It's also scary. You begin to wonder if your darkest secrets are safe. This time, though, I wasn't worried. My conscience was clear. Well, almost clear.

I could see this pie business was bothering her. She was wondering how people can spend a lifetime together and end up knowing so little about one another.

It had her worried. She kept shaking her head in disbelief. I just continued eating my pie.

Actually, it was the first time I had ever done it that way.

Some People Are Driven by Ambition

You'd think she would be supportive. After all, isn't that what a marriage is all about? Aren't husbands and wives supposed to support one another? Didn't I remember something in the wedding ceremony about sickness and health, good times and bad, trials and tribulations, thick and thin, payday to payday?

Those weren't the exact words but it was something like that.
So why, I ask you, did Mrs. H laugh the other day when I revealed to her one of my lifelong ambitions? It isn't that achievement has totally escaped me. Between the two of us we raised four fine children and kept up on the mortgage. No one ever went away from our table hungry. We've tried to be friendly to our neighbors and neighbors to the friendless.

People know what I look like although my face has never been on the bulletin board at the post office. I can cash a check most anywhere in town.

For the last 42 years I've managed to keep gainfully employed, although some of my friends question whether newspapering really qualifies. But I still have an ambition. It's got nothing to do with money. I've been scraping for so long I won't know what to do when the Reader's Digest gives me the $5 million it promised a while back.

Becoming a sex object would be more trouble than it's worth. I've accepted the fact that the Pulitzer Prize Committee isn't paying attention. No one has been around lately suggesting I run for governor.

I do, however, have one last goal—something I've wanted since I was a boy. I don't know why. People shouldn't have to explain their secret dreams. Walter Mitty, the James Thurber character, didn't. He just slipped off into imaginary exploits whenever he had an idle moment.

That's what I do. Every once in a while I find myself dreaming of what it would be like. It's a beautiful dream. It's always the same. Every eye is on me as I stroll briskly out of the terminal. Everyone knows I'm a skilled professional. I'm wearing a natty uniform with brass buttons and gold trim, a pair of Wellington boots and a jaunty cap. There's a pair of aviator sunglasses casually pushed up on my forehead.

My eyes have those little squinty marks men get from years of scanning distant horizons. Everyone knows just by looking that I am of a special breed of men in whom they can entrust their lives.

Mrs. H can't see how important that is to me. Sure, I'm getting old, but not too old to realize one final ambition.

I still want—just once—to drive a bus.

The Bare Truth About Lingerie

There's only one way for a man to walk into the lingerie department of a store—boldly. Never mind the knocking knees. Step up boldly and do what has to be done. It doesn't get easier. That's something I learned as a 12-year old newspaper carrier.

Latimer's Department Store was one of my customers. Latimer specialized in lingerie. His department was in the middle of the main floor.

Lingerie departments, what with corsets, girdles and other paraphernalia then in vogue, were even larger in those days than now.

Latimer's office was at the rear. There was only one way to get there: through lingerie.

Saturday morning collections were to my juvenile mind akin to entering the valley of the shadow of death. I lived in dread of stumbling onto a scantily-clad customer who would, of course, scream and blame me for intruding.

Given the chance I would have gladly traded Latimer and any two people on my route for one nice, uncomplicated residential customer, but none of my buddies were the least bit interested. In retrospect I truly believe those walks through Latimer's lingerie had something to do with my prematurely gray hair.

To this day lingerie departments are my nemesis. I masquerade by walking boldly, but shaky knees give me away. I'm like a horse with blinders—eyes focused straight ahead lest a sideward glance be misinterpreted. Something dreadful usually happens.

The first year we were married I walked into a store where nobody knew me and bought a lovely white nightgown for Mrs. H. I was so proud until I discovered it was three sizes too small and four times too expensive.

Crushed, I said it wouldn't make me angry if she wanted to stop by on her way to work and exchange it.

For 39 years, on the dubious theory that stoically enduring pain builds character, I have made it a practice to be her sole supplier of lingerie.

After that first confidence shattering solo venture, I enlisted advice and help from a trusted female friend on the next gift-giving occasion. Then, for several years, I had an understanding with the woman who ran the lingerie department of a local department store—I bought and she didn't talk.

But one way or the other I have fulfilled my duty despite emotional trauma. I wrote two years ago of the hideous experience of finding a size 10 red bikini floating along behind me on the way out of the lingerie department store. No one—least of all Mrs. H—believed my fervent protestations to the effect it had inadvertently snagged on the sleeve of my coat.

In some respect she is a hard woman. I've known that for years. Not until a couple weeks ago did I realize how hard. She was looking for a summer nightgown—said she was getting tired of the one I had obtained at great emotional expense six or eight years ago.

At the store I behaved fairly well. I didn't drop any garments on the floor, catch anything on my sleeve or see anything untoward. All I did was lean against a large, marble pillar—only it wasn't a large marble pillar. It just looked like one. The thing was made of cardboard.

It rocked like the ruins of Pompeii, jostling a scantily-clad mannequin who started doing the same thing. Both teetered precariously. I managed to steady them just in time. As I took a deep, shuddering breath, someone started laughing. It sounded familiar. It was.

"You almost knocked those over," Mrs. H said between guffaws. "You could have broken that mannequin into a half-dozen pieces."

"I know," I said. "But you'd have helped me pick them up, wouldn't you?"

"Are you kidding?" she said. "I'd have walked away laughing." She would have too.

Lew Hudson

Dispatches From Our Corner of the Globe

Case of the Wandering Lingerie

From time to time in this column I have described some of the idiosyncrasies of the woman who has shared life with me for the last 37 years. Fortunately for me, Mrs. H has a great sense of humor. In fact, to hear her tell it, she didn't realize what a sense of humor she had until we were married.

Anyway, we were talking about that the other day. "A sense of humor," she said, "has always helped me recognize idiosyncrasies when I see them, and around here they don't seem to observe gender boundaries."

"Sometime when you're sick," she continued, "I'm going to write your column and let the whole world judge who has idiosyncrasies and who doesn't."

"I've always been blessed with good health," I quickly pointed out, "but just in case I should get sick, I'd be happy to have you write a column. By the way, where would you start?"

"The case of the wandering lingerie would be as good as any," she replied.

"That," I said, isn't fair. Just because I was carrying that itty bitty, teensy weensy size 10 red bikini sleepwear set out of the lingerie department of one of Brainerd's major department stores back before Christmas doesn't mean I had any intention of buying it or not, for that matter, doing anything else with it."

To which she answered something that sounded like Hummmmph."

"Now don't talk like that," I pleaded. "The little plastic hanger caught the sleeve of my coat as I walked past the rack. I didn't even notice it was stuck on my coat until you called it to my attention."

She said something about Richard Nixon being more believable when he was explaining Watergate but I pressed on.

"It was the store's fault," I said. "They had those display racks jammed so close together, I could hardly squeeze through."

I could feel the noose tightening, but because they usually don't pull the lever while the condemned man is saying his last words, I kept talking.

"Maybe it did look strange," I continued, "but whatever happened to being innocent until proven guilty? Besides, I would have noticed it before you did if, gentleman that I am, I had not averted my eyes as I walked past the rack."

She didn't buy that argument either. Under her breath she muttered something about "flirty old man." At least I think that's what she said. She doesn't always talk so loud as she used to.

Caught red-handed, I'd had no alternative but to return the garment to its rack—which I would have been willing to do, had I known on which rack it belonged. "Help me," I pleaded as I stood there in the aisle.

About that time, this woman who has been my right arm and helpmate for almost four decades suddenly developed total amnesia. "Don't you remember where you picked it up?" she asked sweetly.

To tell the truth, by that time I didn't even recall which state I was in, let alone which rack of filmy garments was minus one of its filmiest numbers.

Then she started laughing and laughed until the tears ran down her face.

I can see I'm going to have to take very good care of my health. Stories like this are bad enough in my own words. Hard telling how they would come out in hers.

The Battle of the Blanket

There's one thing Mrs. H and I agree upon: we wouldn't want to be starting married life again. So many things must be decided and so many adjustments made. We just don't think we're up to it.

Take the matter of the toilet tissue roll, for example. Every married couple has to come to an early understanding of whether it should unroll from the top or the bottom. In the absence of compromise, a marriage between a high roller and a low roller is doomed

Dark versus light toast is another troublemaker. Few toasters can do one slice amber, as I like, and the other dark, as she prefers. We lucked out on this one. Our toaster, known affectionately as Old Smokey, suntans one side and charcoals the other, so we just butter the side we favor and try to ignore what's below.

And coffee. We agreed from the start on the brand and the method of brewing, but it took more than 20 years to mutually conclude that black is beautiful. You can bet we're no strangers to compromise, but there's one stumbling block to marital bliss we have never been able to remove: how should the blankets be placed for sleeping.

All my life I've brought them over my shoulders and tucked them under my chin. But do you suppose she will? Ha! It probably stems from her farm upbringing. The second floor of the house in which she grew up was neither insulated nor heated. She swears in January it was warmer outside.

To prevent frostbite, they pulled the blankets over their heads. That, however, was a long time ago. But still old habits die hard. After four decades, we still can't agree on the blankets.

About the time I get them carefully tucked under my chin, she rolls over, shrugs her shoulder and–zap—they're over my head. I crane my neck and re-tuck them under, my chin whereupon she harrumphs and yanks them out again.

Yank! Jerk! Heave! Haul!

It goes on until one of us gives up. Once she gave up too easily and that made me suspicious. I feigned sleep to see why. Sure enough, just about the time she thought I was gone for the night, she gave a big yank, hiked the covers over her head, sighed profoundly and went to sleep. That's when I decided to get even.

I took up snoring.

Snoring: Annoying Yet Uncontrollable

"It isn't your snoring that bothers me. When you don't, I lie awake."

Mrs. H was talking. I was listening. I'm good at that. It comes with practice. She's not one to complain, but snoring is one subject on which she has long been both vocal and critical. It's not that I'm not sympathetic, but I've maintained a man can't be held responsible for criminal behavior about which he is totally oblivious and over which he has no control.

Unfortunately, that hasn't proved a very successful defense, so over the years I have dutifully commiserated with her. It must be tough trying to sleep in what sounds like a sawmill processing gnarled oak railroad ties containing a few overlooked spikes. "The noise I understand," I said. "The lack of same I don't. Tell me about it."

"I could stand it," she said, "if you were consistent, but you're not. You start quietly and get louder with each breath. Finally when you reach triple fortissimo, you let out a loud pop. Then you hold your breath. It seems to last forever. Time stands still. About the time I begin to wonder if you're still alive, you let out a snort. Then comes the whine—the darndest sound you ever heard, a high-pitched persistent whine. It's eerie. It goes on and on. When it finally stops, the snoring begins all over again."

"That must be tough, " I said, "but it can't be any worse than your dad. I remember when we used to visit at the farm, his snoring sounded like a combination of someone calling hogs and hogs calling back."

"Much worse," she said. I shook my head. "Worse than your brother-in-law?" I asked. This was the brother-in-law whose snoring had been known to lift shingles on the roof. "Yep," she said.

"Worse even than robins in the tree outside the window at 3:30 a.m.?" That got her. "Well, I don't know," she said. "Louder—yes—but worse? I'm not sure."

It wasn't really a fair question. Few things are as bad as the monotonous pre-dawn dirge of a family of tone-deaf robins. The noise, seemingly subdued at first, has a way of increasing in intensity if not actual volume. It bores into the victim's mind, inexorably dragging the subconscious to full alertness.

It's something like Chinese water torture where the psychological impact of tiny drops of water falling on the forehead increases steadily until the victim eventually goes bonkers.

"It's frightful," I said.

"You're right," she agreed. "As bad as your snoring is, it doesn't hold a candle to the predawn chirp of robins."

"I tell you what we'll do," I said. "Next time we come home late at night, let's wander around the yard meowing like cats and wake all the robins up. That'll pay 'em back for all those sleepless dawns."

"I'd love to," she said, "but how would we explain it to the neighborhood?"

Why Do They Put Pockets in Pajamas?

What are pajama pockets for? That's been nagging at me for a long time. Every pair of pajamas I ever owned had a pocket, but I've never used one. The other day I took the question to the Oracle of Ashdale Lane. "What," I asked her, "are pajama pockets for?"

"They're for men who smoke cigarettes in bed," she replied.

"Naw," I said. "Who'd put cigarette ashes in their pajama pockets?"

"Not for ashes," she said, "for cigarette packets."

"Wrong again," I said. "Every roll-over would pulverize a pack of expensive cigarettes into cheap snoose."

"I give up," she said. "You tell me."

They're surely not for ballpoint pens. Nobody in his right mind would sleep with a ballpoint pen in his pocket. A pair of glasses wouldn't last long. A candy bar would melt. A fellow doesn't need credit cards in bed. Pocket knives and combs could be dangerous to your health. A handkerchief? Naw. Not many guys wear pocket handkerchiefs anymore and those that do wear 'em in the pocket of their suit coats.

Just think of the material, thread and time wasted making pajama pockets. While the amount individually is small, the collective drain on the Gross National Product must be substantial. If pajama companies eliminated pockets they'd probably save enough they wouldn't have to move their factories into cheap labor markets overseas. Just think of the jobs saved.

Where do George Bush and Patrick Buchanan stand on this issue? What about Bill Clinton, Paul Tsongas and Jerry Brown? Has Jesse Jackson taken a position? Do Eugene McCarthy and Harold Stassen have an opinion? They've had plenty of time to think about it.

The fact of the matter is this: the United States of America needs to either start using pajama pockets or get rid of them. They're either necessary or they're not. Wasn't it Abraham Lincoln who said a house divided against itself—half slave to pajama pockets and half free—cannot long stand?

Mark my words. It's only a matter of time until some civil rights activist discovers that men have pajama pockets and women don't, and then you know what'll happen. Some lawyer with a reputation for getting into deep pockets will file a sexual discrimination lawsuit and women's gowns will soon be required to have pockets just like men's pajamas do now.

Just think what that's going to mean to the lingerie business. Prices will go up. Sales will go down. You'll have fewer pennies to put in your pajama pockets.

Assuming, of course, that's where you keep them.

Zzzz the Battle for Some Blissful Sleep

There are times when Mrs. H considers that childhood ear infection one of the best things that ever happened to her. It left her right ear weaker than her left. So when I start snoring she just puts her good ear in the pillow and makes the best of a bad situation.

There's no denying the fact it's noisy. I come from a long line of sound sleepers. My grandfather was a regional champion. My dad could thunder just as loud from the bedroom at night as he did from the pulpit on Sundays.

The beat goes on. Last fall when my three brothers were in town for a fishing trip the windows were rattling and jack pines shaking like quaking aspens all over the neighborhood.

I used to think Mrs. H exaggerated the racket until I hung a sound activated tape recorder on the bedpost one night and listened to the result. It was awesome. That tape became one of the kids' favorite comedy albums.

Of late, though, I've been getting some competition. Far be it from me to suggest that anyone else around our house snores. That wouldn't be gentlemanly. Let's just say that we both breathe a little more audibly than we used to. Which means there are now two contestants in the race to get to sleep first.

It's a tricky game. The idea is to plant a nagging thought in the other person's mind without letting on what you're doing. Done right it can buy five minutes of blissful silence during which—if you're lucky—you can get to sleep. It has to be done carefully though.

Overplay your hand and you run the risk of getting your own mind cranked up and that defeats the purpose. There are some rules. No surreptitious substituting of regular for decaf coffee. No politics or TV talk show discussions. No talking about relatives after 9 p.m.

Just about everything else is OK. It's a game of punch and counter punch. The more devious the better. You don't want to be obvious. The secret is to casually mention something that is irksome enough to attain the desired effect without stirring much in the way of a reply.

It's a tough balancing act. To the victors belong the spoils: a good night's sleep.

Mrs. H Controls the Rationing

"I'll just take the maraschino cherry," she said. Mrs. H was opening a can of fruit cocktail and spooning it into a couple dessert dishes. As usual, there was only one cherry in the whole can. I didn't argue. I would have if it had been a can of pork and beans. Pork is worth arguing about. I'm a veteran of hundreds of who-gets-the-pork arguments.

Only one piece to a can—the smaller the better—is the industry rule. Occasionally there is a chunk an inch or so square, but usually it's just a little dab.

I saw a cartoon once in a magazine showing a huge pork and bean factory. There was a little pen out back with two scrawny hogs. The cartoon showed a company executive escorting a visitor around the factory saying, "Yes, we raise all our own pork."

Who got the pork was serious business when I was growing up. More than once, my brothers and I argued so long and hard about it that our mother had to intervene. If you think that's bad, you should have been around when our four youngsters were at home and Mrs. H fried a chicken.

Four kids and two drumsticks is a recipe for a hassle. Fortunately, chickens also have two thighs, which opens room for negotiation. "I'll trade you a thigh and a wing for your drumstick." "Throw in a gizzard and it's yours."

When it came to the heart, though, there was no room for bargaining. The heart is the heart of the chicken. I swear those kids kept score. They could rattle off who got the heart for the previous 12 months. I've seen Mrs. H surgically divide one into six equal pieces just to keep all of us—herself included—happy.

One time, when I thought no one was looking, I sneaked the heart off the platter and popped it in my mouth. I was feeling pretty smug until I looked up to see five pairs of accusing eyes looking at me like I had pawned the family jewels.

Sharing can be ticklish. Dividing a pie or cake into equal portions calls for the sort of precision best accomplished by letting one person do the cutting and the others do the choosing.

Mrs. H grew up on a farm and a cream pitcher was on the table at every meal. Not so at our house. Our milk came from the dairy in what were called cream-top bottles. Since milk wasn't homogenized, the cream rose to the top and collected in the bulbous neck, where it, presumably, was to be shared equally.

That's a laugh. Presuming and doing were different things. By the time the bottle got around to me, only skim milk was left. My brother, Hawkeye Bob, even figured out a way to cheat on sugar. During sugar-rationing days of World War II, we had a firm rule—only one teaspoon to a bowl of cereal.

Hawkeye would hold the sugar bowl over his cereal, dig his spoon in and "unintentionally" spill some over the side. I saw him do it hundreds of times. He always denied doing it on purpose. I'll bet he still would. Next time I see him, I'm going to see what he says about it now.

But about that maraschino cherry, there wasn't any reason to argue about it. It wouldn't have done any good. The person who dibs first around our house usually wins, and Mrs. H clearly spoke first. Besides, a fellow can afford to be magnanimous when he doesn't particularly like maraschino cherries.

Mrs. H Won't Reveal Her Secret

One look at her and I could tell something was wrong. Her face was pale and drawn. Worry lines scored her forehead. A frown perched lightly on the edges of her lips. She was uncommonly quiet.

Mrs. H was not her normal morning self.

"What's wrong?" I asked. She slowly shook her head. "I had a terrible nightmare. It scared me half to death."

"Tell me about it," I said. "That always seems to help."

"I was dreaming I had just weighed myself on the bathroom scales," she said. "But the reading was wrong. Then as I started to tell you about it I almost gave away the secret. I caught myself just in time."

Communication is important in a marriage. Marriage counselors encourage husbands and wives to share openly with one another. Mrs. H and I have always done so—well, most of the time. The book doesn't say couples have to tell every deep, dark secret about themselves.

On some things, though, she absolutely refuses to play by the rules. For 38 years prior to this coming January 4, she has steadfastly refused to tell me how much she weighs.

It's not that weight is a forbidden subject. She's always happy to tell me when she manages to lose three or four pounds. Once in a while she even tells me when she's had a bad weekend and picked up a couple, but the net total is top secret.

I have tried reasoning, argument, threats, deceit and bribery—all to no avail. If I knew hypnotism I'd try that.

Once I was going to pick up her fishing license at the courthouse and casually asked what weight I should put down. She told me it was none of my business.

I explained that, down at the bottom where I would have to sign, there is some fine print about swearing the above information is accurate and true under penalty of law. I emphasized those last words: UNDER PENALTY OF LAW. She said she hoped the judge wouldn't deal too harshly with me.

I did the best I could under the circumstances but apparently guessed a little high. I almost froze to death at the supper table that night.

Another time I asked a friend who worked at the driver's license bureau what weight Mrs. H listed on her license. I could have guessed how that would turn out.

Weight of a licensee, I was told is privileged information and even if it wasn't, they wouldn't tell me without clearing first with Mrs. H.

Once for $5 I even hired our daughter Cindy to weasel out the vital statistics. It didn't take Mrs. H two hours to get wind of what was afoot, and the deal fell flat on its face.

I grabbed her one time in the bathroom, hoping to pick her up and step quickly on the scales. That, friends, was not one of my better ideas.

In desperation once, I worked out a deal with the guy who ran the truck scales out at the Farmer's Elevator. It was a great scheme. I said I'd drive up with her in the car. He said he'd give me a fast reading before she had time to get out and run. Knowing the gross total, it would have been simple mathematics to get a second weighing, subtract and arrive at the coveted answer.

It didn't work. When I suggested we go for a ride, she wouldn't even get in the car—said she had a headache.

One of my cronies suggested I get four bathroom scales and

sneak one under each corner of her bed. From the combination of all four readings, we reasoned, it should be possible to calculate the sleeper's weight. We must have had a bunch of blabby people running garage sales in the neighborhood. I had only bought two before she got wind of the deal and put me out of the scale business fast.

Her hand trembled a bit as she picked up her coffee cup. There were beads of cold sweat on her forehead. "What a nightmare," she said. "I stopped myself just as I was saying one hundred and ..." Her voice trailed off.

"A hundred and what?" I asked.

"No way, Jose," she snapped.

Lew Hudson

Top Rated Shows Are Never Watched

It took the Nielsen Rating Service to make liars of us. The invitation came in the mail—our first, last and probably only chance for a place in the national sun.

"Would you be willing to be one of our Nielsen households for a week?" the letter asked. "It is people like you," it continued, "who help decide what appears on television. Ratings that the various programs receive go a long way toward deciding what types of programs will be offered in the future."

A chance to influence television programming? Someone was going to pay attention to what we thought about TV? We leaped at the chance. All we had to do was keep a log of our TV viewing for one week and send it to the company. In return, we could keep the modest sum of money included with the letter.

And that's when the lying began. I was first.

Dialing across the spectrum, I stopped to watch the tail end of a wrestling match between a fellow who resembled a wet hippopotamus and a blonde-haired ape with a fresh permanent. It was just getting interesting—the hippo had his thumb in the ape's nose and his fingers in his eyes, trying to convert his head into a bowling ball, while the ape was applying a double ankle bend to the hippo's left foot and kneeing him in the groin. Both were groaning like there wasn't going to be a tomorrow.

"Don't forget to log the program," Mrs. H called from the kitchen. Now, if you think I'm going to let some yahoo in New York know that I watch professional wrestling, you've got another think coming.

I logged it as 30 minutes of a public television presentation of a 17th century Italian folk play performed with English subtitles.

Mrs. H was just as bad. Three hours of soaps magically became three hours of nature programs, cooking demonstrations by a home economist and discussions on international trade by a team of economists from Harvard, Princeton and the University of Notre Dame.

Between the two of us, by the end of the week we had logged more hours of uplifting TV than any two persons could possibly stomach in a month. And we weren't the slightest bit remorseful. In fact, by week's end we found we could lie without flinching or even thinking about it. While our eyes watched sleaze, our hands recorded culture.

Geraldo became Dan Rather. "Days of Our Lives" became "Masterpiece Theatre." "Roller Derby" became "The NFL Today." Sue Ellen of "Dallas" became Mona Lisa of Paris. Matt Dillon became Billy Graham. Phil Donahue was listed as Louis Rukeyser. Dr. Ruth came out as Dr. Schuler.

And why not? Would you really admit before God and your fellow human beings the stupid things you watch on TV? Of course not. Faced with recording your TV viewing, you'd do exactly the same as we did.

Your logbook would show nothing but news, nature and nostalgia instead of the nonsense, nastiness and nebulosity you really watch. Tell the truth now. Wouldn't it?

Wallpapering Tests Marriage

If you tend to be emotional, you probably shouldn't read any further. This is a story about wallpapering with the one you love—a subject with enough pathos to wring tears from a turnip.

It's not that Mrs. H and I didn't know better. We once wallpapered a whole house together. Our marriage survived—barely. This time, though, it was just a bathroom. How could two sensible, mature people get into trouble wallpapering a bathroom? Bathrooms are no biggy.

I won't go into details. Suffice it to say that four hands smoothing wallpaper do not contribute to straight seams, that a wallpaper strip someone mistakenly cut 44.5 inches cannot be stretched to cover 45 and that the person working the low end of the strip invariably will complain of being pasted.

If ever a room needed re-papering, this one did. I managed to put it off for three years, but eventually Mrs. H put her foot down. You have no idea how much pressure she can exert. So we began.

Why do inanimate objects always put up such a fight? Stripping that old paper was horrible. We ended up with skinned knuckles, frayed nerves and the darndest mess you ever saw. What's more, the wall had so many scars it had to be re-plastered. Fortunately I had learned the plasterer's art the other time we got into wallpapering. This time it took only three coats and about 50 pounds of mix to get a reasonably smooth surface.

Once that was dry, Mrs. H put on the sizing and we set Saturday morning as wallpaper day. Saturday is the best day for wallpapering. That's because Saturday is followed by Sunday and most churches provide a time during worship for confessing sins. Because of the events of Saturday, we both had goodly lists.

We're getting along better now. Time has a way of healing. Marriage counselors should have a wallpaper warning session with each pair of clients. Young couples need to know what they face if they take up wallpapering—basic things like the following:

- -No matter how much wallpaper you buy, you will always be one roll   short.
- -The only rolls remaining in stock will be from a different dye lot.
- -Dye lots never match.
- -The place where the first batch ends and last begins will be the most visible point in the room.
- -20 percent of each roll will be waste.
- -No blade is keen enough to cut wet wallpaper.

Mrs. H Can Knit Up a Storm

Some things I just don't understand. For example:
-How the little steel balls in pen points can be produced so cheaply.
-How pocket calculators work.
-How digital watch images are projected.
-Knitting.
The first three I may someday learn. The last is beyond me. Mrs. H has been a knitter since before we were married. I remember buying her a knitting book at Carson Pirie Scott in Chicago when we were honeymooning. She still has it.

Over the years her needles have produced an unending stream of mittens, scarves, hats, sweaters, vests, ponchos and other items of apparel. She's one of the few women in the world who looked forward to her children losing a mitten because it gave her an excuse to make another pair.

The other evening she started a headband for one of our granddaughters at 9:30 p.m. and finished it before Paul Douglas completed the weather report on the evening news.

The week before she was working on an afghan for our daughter's birthday. That of course took a bit longer. It was an

Indian blanket design involving about four colors.

Night after night she hummed along contentedly. When the knitting was done she spent three evenings tying off the ends complaining all the while it was driving her batty. She didn't fool me. She enjoyed herself all the way.

At that it was simpler than the snowflake sweater she did a few years ago. That one involved about a dozen little spindles to hold the different yarns. From where I was sitting it looked like she was eating spaghetti with chopsticks.

She says she's willing to teach me to knit anytime I'm up to it. So far I'm not. There are some things that are beyond the male intellect. Knitting is one. Crocheting is another. Mrs. H says she doesn't like crocheting. It's too simple.

Every time she talks like that I remember visiting the Faribault State Hospital many years ago. In one of the craft rooms I saw a half completed bit of breathtakingly beautiful lace. It was an incredibly intricate design fed by as many as 30 or 40 spindles.

I asked an attendant whose work it was.

"One of our residents," she said.

"How long will it take her to finish it?" I asked.

"It will never be done," I was told. "The woman died and there is no one here who knows the pattern."

She went on to explain it was an ancient design from Belgium. The woman who had started it was profoundly retarded in every way except lacework. In that she was a genius.

Never before or since have I seen lacework the equal of it. For all I know it may still be there waiting for someone with the ability to complete it. I guess I should add lacework to the list of things I will never understand. That and Mrs. H.

Mrs. H Gets Her Chance to Tell All

If I've said it once I've said it a hundred times—people just don't know what I have to endure. Now at last I'm going to tell.

For years I've threatened to write a guest column—a threat that has prompted Mr. H to be very careful about the state of his health. This week, though, he slipped. He spent most of the week in Duluth covering a trial and his column for today didn't get written. I jumped at the chance to help out. One column won't set the whole record straight but it'll help.

First, let's deal with the matter of editorial license. That's what he calls it when he's writing about me. "Never let the facts get in the way of a good story," he says. Editorial license? Editorial lying, I call it.

I'm not like him. I write plain, unvarnished facts.

He snores. Not just snores, mind you, but snores like a band saw hitting an embedded railroad spike. Friends advised twin beds. They didn't help. With him, twin houses wouldn't be enough. But come morning, there's not a sound. For 38 years I've led this mute hunk of humanity from the bedroom to the kitchen, sat him down at his accustomed spot, handed him a glass of orange juice and waited patiently for a word or two of greeting. Ha! The Sphinx talks more than he does at breakfast.

After breakfast it's nap time. A half-hour. I can set my watch by it. Then, and only then, is he ready to go out and face the world—more or less. It's a good thing he faces it. If he depended on his ears he'd never know what was going on. The man is deaf as a post. He even talks to posts sometimes.

We pulled up to a drive-in restaurant last summer. They had a loud-speaker system to call in your order. "Two ice cream cones," he said. "Vanilla," he said. "I wanted vanilla." The post broke into laughter. He didn't hear.

In everything but politics he's a mule. Stubborn? Set in his ways? Not to hear him tell it. He says he's just trying to persuade the rest of the world to see things right for a change.

I like crossword puzzles. He doesn't. But when I'm momentarily perplexed, he invariably offers his help. Big deal! That man's got more imagination than word skill. If he doesn't know the word he makes one up and tries to palm it off on me.

"Absent-minded" is a good description. He misplaces things right and left and then blissfully sits in his recliner, expecting them to parade past him. His favorite poem is the nursery rhyme, "Leave them alone and they'll come home wagging their tails behind them."

In self-defense, I've learned to enjoy football, basketball and hockey. Otherwise there wouldn't be much to do around our house between October and May. Summer is better now that he's begun to learn the secrets of fishing. I've been struggling to teach him for years. "Slow learner," I think is the proper description.

Color-blind? This man would happily wear a purple tie with blue trousers and orange socks if I'd let him. Also, he's inclined toward procrastination. He says if he ever gets around to it he'll do something about it.

When we lived in Worthington, we took out a home improvement loan to build a family room in the basement. The day he put the ceiling tiles up, I made the mistake of calling him to supper with three tiles left to go. Twenty years later, long after the loan had been paid off, he finally put those last three tiles in place. He said it might help the realtor sell the place.

He tells everyone that he's a woodcarver. It's more accurate to say he has been a woodcarver. In the last 10 years he's carved a total of about a day and one half and talked about it the rest.

When we travel he's our restaurant and motel picker. That has produced some doozies. Some days, when I feel devilish, I sneak up behind him and whisper, "Buena Vista Motel," just to watch him cringe. The Buena Vista was in Chattanooga, Tennessee. He pulled into the Howard Johnson first but, predictably, balked when they told him it would cost $27.50 for the six of us. So, across the street we went to the Buena Vista—a place with hammocks masquerading as beds and all kinds of company on the other side of what passed for walls.

By 5 a.m. we'd had it and got up. Our fearless leader said we'd drive an hour or two and stop for breakfast. "Yas suh, boss."

We pulled into a state line café and ordered orange juice. "Ain't got none." Eggs? "Ain't got none." Cereal? "Ain't got none." Coffee? "Ain't..."

We left. It was obviously something other than a café. Whatever brand of moon shine they were selling from the backroom we weren't buying... As we walked out, I chalked up another one for the man of the house. After 38 years it's quite a list.

"Love, honor and obey," the preacher said. Two out of three ain't bad. Don't tell him, but I had my fingers crossed.

Lew Hudson

Chapter 2

Family Reflections

Through the years Dad has called up many an emotional issue in his writing, heaping humor generously on his readers or tugging gently at their hearts. Perhaps the single most poignant subjects to be touched upon are those involving family and loved ones, and these are the stories that will forever remain dear to us all. Sometimes they are not easy to read and may cause a tear to fill your eye, but you will be forever touched by the words. Or you may chuckle with glee and shake your head because you are reminded of such a time in your past. Whatever the case, you will be moved by his humor and straightforward presentation.

Lew Hudson

Confessions of a Former Den Daddy

I'm a former Brownie Papa and Cub Scout Den Daddy, and my heart went out recently to the Brainerd professional man who told me he had volunteered to take over his son's Cub Scout den. The poor man has no conception of what lies in store.

Mrs. H and I know. She put three daughters through Brownies and Girl Scouts before son Fred came along, whereupon she took on what was called a den of Cubs but which was really more like a pack of wolves. Throughout the process, I stood ready to throw my shoulder to the wheel whenever things started to bog down in a morass of mischief.

Mining clay deposits for Brownie handicraft projects, assisting with Brownie fishing trips, helping with Girl Scout parade floats and providing transportation hither and thither wasn't so bad. Camping was. Mention that word around our house and Mrs. H instinctively reacts like a whipped dog. Memories are still too fresh I guess.

We only did it twice—once with the Brownies and once with the Cubs. The Brownie outing was an overnight excursion to a glorified swamp that passed for a lake two miles south of town. Weather was beautiful when they set up camp late in the afternoon by the water's edge. I say that because it has a bearing on what followed.

I stayed home with our youngest daughter, Rebecca, then only three or four years old. Clouds were gathering in the western sky when I put her to bed for the night about 9 p.m. When the 10 p.m. news came on, the announcer started things off with a special weather advisory accompanied by a live radar report blinking like a theater marquee.

Grabbing Rebecca from bed, I ran to the car and started out to save the Brownies. At the lake all was reasonably quiet, and Mrs. H was loath to change that. Against my best advice she stubbornly said, "We'll stick it out."

Before leaving I moved their car out of the lowland. Otherwise it would have been there until freeze-up. It stormed from about midnight until dawn. One little Brownie almost floated out of the tent; another nearly drowned while sleeping on her back beneath a hole in the tent.

We thought it was a hectic night—but that was before we took the Cubs camping. There were 10 of them. Our destination was a county park. When we got there, the park superintendent was surprisingly quick to accept my suggestion that we locate our camp about 300 yards from the regular campground. "Maybe 400 would be better," he said.

I set up a 9-by-18-foot tent for the boys and a pup tent for Mrs. H and myself. Daughter Rebecca, then in high school, rolled out a sleeping bag in the back of the station wagon.

We got camp set up about 5:30 p.m. and opened a can of stew for supper. Chow call was 6 p.m. Kids rolled in from every direction.

One was already muddy clear to his knees. "Looks like quick mud to me," I said. "You're lucky to be alive." "Yeah," he replied.

From that time until taps at 9 p.m. that end of the park gave the appearance of being populated by a gang of gnomes fighting off a swarm of bees. It was constant frenzy.

At 9 p.m. we rounded them up, sent them to the restroom and ordered them confined to the tent until morning.

That was a laugh. For a while they stayed within but the tent was rocking like a sailing ship in a hurricane. Muffled thuds, thumps, uffs, snickers, guffaws, slaps, giggles, yells and shouts emanated in waves.

Within the first half hour three kids with weak bladders applied for potty passes. Two more applied in the following 15 minutes.

Toward 10 p.m. Mrs. H and I retired to the pup tent. Over the din coming from the dormitory I had just said that "I wish we had put our tent a hundred yards or so farther away," when lights of an approaching pickup lighted the camp. It was the park superintendent.

"I just got a call from the hospital in town," he said. "Your daughter Cynthia has suffered an attack of appendicitis. They don't think they'll have to operate but plan to keep her in overnight."

We decided there was nothing we could do about it and since she was in good hands, we'd just stay put. About 30 minutes later we were just about asleep when the superintendent drove up again. "They're taking her into surgery," he said.

It was time for action. We dressed, went into the big tent, told the boys what had happened and ordered them to put on their clothes immediately but to leave everything else exactly where it was because we were breaking camp.

The park superintendent agreed to deliver each boy to his home, and we headed for the hospital, arriving just as the doctor finished surgery. Next morning we went back to the pathetic debris that had been our happy campsite. By late afternoon I had delivered it all to its rightful owners.

I have only one thing to say to the new Brainerd Den Daddy. "Have you really thought this over?"

Lew Hudson

Some Baptisms Aren't So Serene

There was an infant baptism two or three Sundays ago at the Presbyterian Church where Mrs. H and I are members. It was beautiful. The pastor took the child from his parents, placed it on his arm, chucked it under the chin a time or two to get a smile and performed the ceremony. Then he took a stroll up the center aisle to show the child to the congregation, reminding the people of their responsibility to nurture it in the faith. The baby cooed the entire way.

I looked at Mrs. H and smiled. She looked at me and shrugged her shoulders. We didn't speak. We didn't have to. Both of us remember the grim event in our family that has come to be known as "The Baptism of Rebecca".

Our daughter Rebecca was a quiet child. Whenever possible she preferred to avoid confrontation. Given a choice, she'd step aside and let others go first. She was loathe to hurt anyone's feelings. Her voice was quiet, her temper subdued, her demeanor calm— except on the day she was baptized.

We could sense it coming. She was restless during early portions of the service, as if she knew something was amiss. As we carried her to the front of the church, we could see her jaw stiffen and her lower lip protrude. When we handed her to the pastor, she took a deep breath and the fight was on.

She kicked, squirmed, arched her back, clenched her fists, flopped her arms, twisted her body, threw her head back and forth —and when that didn't work, cut loose with blood-curdling screams.

The pastor tried every trick he had learned in 25 years of ministry. He dipped his finger in the baptismal font and moistened her lips, he tried to use his little finger as a pacifier, he sat her upright in his arms, he chucked her under the chin, he smiled at her, he bounced her up and down—and she yelled all the louder.

Finally, seeing he wasn't getting anywhere, he went ahead with the ceremony, despite the din. The way she was kicking and screaming, it was all he could do to keep from dropping her.

She was still going strong when he finished the ceremony and handed her back to her mother, whereupon of course, she promptly quieted down.

When the echoes quit reverberating, the pastor ruefully told the congregation he hoped God had heard what had been said because he was sure no one in the church did. Later he told us privately it was the loudest baptism he had ever performed.

Poor guy. He had no way of knowing what fate had in store for him. Six years later, along came Fred. By comparison to Fred, Rebecca was a pacifist. He started yelling bloody murder right after the opening hymn. When we went to the front of the church and turned to face the people, he cranked up the volume to what old timers in that church swore was a new record.

Not long after that the pastor resigned and took a new church out West somewhere. I don't think the two events were related, but you never can tell. Since that time Mrs. H and I have witnessed dozens upon dozens of baptisms. Occasionally a child fusses a bit but for the most part, the infants are content, the parents proud and the minister pleased.

Every time it happens I look over at Mrs. H and smile. She looks at me and shrugs her shoulders. And we both remember a different time and a different place when our two children set marks that may live forever in the annals of Presbyterianism.

Ugly Side of the Rainbow

It sounds so innocent. A Rainbow Family reunion. Word is that it will be held this summer in either the Chippewa or Superior National Forest in northern Minnesota. The Cass County Board got the news Tuesday.
What is a Rainbow Family reunion? Just a group of 10,000 or so people coming together to camp, sing, reminisce, laugh, enjoy each other and commune with nature. At least that's what they told a young man from Tennessee at the time of their 1987 reunion.
It was held in the Nantahala National Forest near Asheville, N.C. The crowd was variously estimated between 5,000 and 12,000. Details of what was said to him and who said it are hazy. Even his parents never got the straight of it.
All they remember is that Deano came home one evening and told them he had been invited to spend a few days camping and hiking in the North Carolina Mountains. Sort of a reunion, he said.
It sounded like fun. He went. He came home a shattered man.
Deano was no stranger to drugs. He smoked a little marijuana once in a while—made no bones about it. But he was afraid of hard drugs. He had seen what they did to his older brother. Never used them, he said, and there was no reason to doubt his word.

But when he came home from the Rainbow Family reunion, he was obviously in a drug-induced dream world. He wandered back and forth between reality and illusion. In his more rational moments he agonized over the plight of the children at the Rainbow Family camp.

When less rational, he spoke of being told by people at the camp to go home, get $10,000 and bring it back to them. Otherwise, he said, they were going to kill his parents.

Or was it the other way around? Which was the rational and which the irrational story? No one could tell for sure where Deano's reality ended and illusion began, nor could anyone identify the drug that had induced his agonizing trip. But he was obviously under extreme mental duress. At one point he told his father he could not live with what he had seen at the camp.

He spoke the truth. A short time later he went to his room, loaded a shotgun and killed himself. Was it just a bad drug trip or had Deano observed behavior beyond normal boundaries?

Did the Rainbow Family send out recruits to induce young people to come up to the mountain? Who put up the money for a 5,000-person encampment? Who did the logistical planning? Who dug the latrines? Who laid out the campsites? And why?

Was it just for a reunion of burned-out hippies and drop-out potheads, or was there a more sinister motivation?

Who was supplying the hard drugs so freely circulating around the camp? Who was profiting from them? Was someone mixing the more dangerous ones with marijuana and giving it to the impressionable young people?

Did someone implant into their drug-warped minds demands for money or services? Was that the source of Deano's torment—a torment so real he concluded he had to kill himself to remove the threat to his parents?

These questions and more have been discussed by his family ever since. There are no answers. There is only a shattered life to look back upon—and another Rainbow Family reunion to anticipate. How do I know these things? A fair question. Deano was my nephew.

Dispatches From Our Corner of the Globe

VW Beetle Kept Kids from Walking

If it hadn't been for the VW Beetle our kids would have had to walk their way through high school and college. Beetles were the only thing in the way of transportation that was cheap enough to keep 'em rolling.

In my own fiscal self-defense when I bought our first VW, a repair manual was also part of the deal. With it in one hand and a set of metric tools in the other, I managed to keep wheels under the kids and a dollar or two in my bank account during those lean years.

There wasn't anything very complicated about a Beetle. Four cylinders and a single throat carburetor is pretty straight forward stuff. You could time the distributor by guess and by gosh if you had to but even if you wanted to be precise about it all you needed was a flashlight bulb and a couple lengths of wire.

Only four bolts held the engine in place. By the third time I pulled an engine I could have one lying on the garage floor ready to dismantle in 43 minutes flat. Putting it back in took longer. About an hour and a half, as I recall. You could change oil in four minutes if you cheated a bit and didn't pull the screen for cleaning. The design that made that possible however, had its drawbacks. In winter, should the thermostat stop working, condensation would form water which would in turn freeze to ice and block the oil intake screen. So if you cheated too often by not cleaning the screen you had to drive with one eye on the pressure light because if it came on you could blow an engine in minutes.

Changing oil was cheap. It only took two and one half quarts. The ball joints, tie rod ends and related pieces were lifetime lubricated (something General Motors still hadn't learned to do the last time I looked under one of its cars).

What's more, simply by lying on your back on the front seats of a Beetle you could look up under the dash and correct anything wrong with the entire electrical system. Try that in a modern Ford or Chrysler.

To be sure Beetles had their drawbacks. Leg room wasn't one of their strong points but on the other hand when you folded down the rear seat you could get a surprising amount inside. One time my daughters LuAnn and Cynthia, who between the two of them made up two thirds of the high school orchestra's violin section, got themselves, a violist, and a string bass player, all with their instruments, into a Beetle called "Willy" for a trip across town from one school to another.

Willy got his name, incidentally, from the first overhaul I gave him. "Will he run or won't he. That is the question." Shakespeare never said it better.

I bought Willy for $50 and a used trailer hitch. He turned in 17,000 miles before an advanced case of rust (we called it consumption) set in. We put him out of his misery after someone put their foot through his floor.

A replacement Beetle cost $35. The guy who had it thought it had thrown a rod. It sounded like it, all right. Unfortunately for him this guy didn't know Beetles. I did.

It sounded to me like a case of a rocker arm stud pulling through, only I didn't say anything to him about it until after he had mulled over the offer of $35 cash, "as she stands". He went away happy with the $35. I spent $8 bucks for a rocker arm sleeve and my youngest daughter drove that car more than 50,000 miles over the next three years after which we sold it for $250 when it too developed a serious case of consumption.

Altogether we had three Beetles, two Karmann Ghias, a 411 and finally an Audi (which ate more money than gasoline). Throughout, I developed an admiration for the basic honesty of Ferdinand Porsche's original Beetle design. It was straight forward, honest and cheap. Small wonder it was produced for more than 35 years.

What's more it was built with the mechanic in mind. While working quarters were cramped, everything could be reached by one mechanic working alone. Now contrast that with the Austin Healy sports car to which my son developed an emotional attachment. The English make beautiful sports cars even though they seemingly don't know how to make weather-tight bodies on them. A fellow could live with that though if it weren't for the engineering. Unlike Beetles where everything is out in the open within reach, every adjustment on the Austin is located in such a way as to require a double jointed mechanic with a full set of swivel wrenches.

Maybe that's why they made 15,000,000 Beetles and only around 200,000 or so Austins. But I have to admit the Austin has better lines. And when you're 19 and in love with a car, who wants to be practical?

Lew Hudson

The Father of the Bride

It has been said that the father of a bride should show up at his daughter's wedding, shut up and pay up. No one is very interested in his opinion on the proper color for a bridesmaid's dress or what the caterer should serve at the reception. No one asks whether he prefers a traditional black tuxedo or one of those passionate pink or powder blue models seen so often these days.

Details such as singers, attendants, flowers, seating arrangements, reception lines, punch bowls, ceremonies, Scripture, candles, cake, silver service, music and who does what are clearly the province of someone else.

Seemingly the only people interested in the father of the bride are his banker and the vendors of wedding supplies. It's the only time in his life that he is expected to hand over his wallet to perfect strangers, letting them take whatever they want.

There is, however, more to it than that. Three times it has been my privilege to be father of the bride. Three times I have stood at the end of an aisle alongside a girl suddenly grown to womanhood, awaiting the signal to take one of life's longest walks.

Three times tears have filled my eyes as recollections of growing up years flooded my mind. Three times I have pondered what to say in those last, fleeting moments.

It is a time of deep frustration. More than anything else the father of the bride wants happiness for his daughter, but it is no longer his to give. He wants to see her protected, but that is now someone else's job. He wants to go on clearing stones out of her path, but now she wants to climb over them with someone else. He wants to be needed, but today she needs someone else.

And, when the end of the aisle is reached, neither will he be needed again. So what does the father of the bride say to his beloved daughter? She already knows right from wrong. She already knows what it is to love and be loved as a human being. She has already weighed the advantages and disadvantages of marriage and decided her course of action. She has already calculated the economics of family life and drawn up a positive balance sheet.

It would seem an appropriate time to say something, but what is an appropriate thing to say at a time like this? How about it, father of the bride? This is your last opportunity to share something with your daughter while you are still her number one man. Each of the three times I have stood there, I have known what I wanted to say. I have wanted to share with her the secrets of marriage I learned through the years of experience.

I wanted to say, "My beautiful daughter, now that you've made your decision don't ever look back. There is no room in life for second-guessing. Keep your eyes on distant goals. Learn from your mistakes. Discard guilt because it is an impossible burden. Become your husband's best friend. Develop common interests because love alone will not sustain you. Respect one another. Keep your sense of humor."

That's what I have wanted to say, only I didn't. There wasn't time. There never was. There was only time for a glance into her eyes and a smile through the tears. And then, "Take my arm daughter. They're waiting for us." That's what I ended up saying. Not very original, was it? But I think they understood.

Some private thoughts by the father of the bride: Was her mother ever that young?...Bouquets cost what?...They're lovers now. Hope they become good friends, too...A white aisle cloth costs how much?...You want how much per person for a reception?...Ragweed must be bad this year, my eyes keep watering...I'd have saved money if I'd bought a tux when the first one was married...I think more is being spent on film for this one than our whole wedding cost...She was my shy, quiet one. When did her backbone turn to tempered steel?...Who gives this woman... Her mother and I do—our most treasured possession and now she's yours.

Lew Hudson

Travels Without Kids: Ah, the Peace and Quiet

Not long ago Mrs. H and I had occasion to drive to Iowa City. It's 450 miles from here to there—eight solid hours of driving—but we didn't think much about it. We put our Thermos pumper of coffee in its customary place between the seats, laid in a supply of cookies to stave off stray hunger pangs and took off.

I drove the first shift. At Albert Lea we made a fuel and rest stop and she took over for the run on to Iowa City. Along the way we talked, watched the world go by and listened to the stereo. Each of us even dozed a bit while the other was driving.

It was not always so. We used to travel with children. That's not to say our kids weren't good travelers. They were, but traveling with kids even under the best conditions is not one of life's more pleasurable activities.

It wasn't so bad at first. When she was an only child, LuAnn roamed the back seat, entertaining herself most of the time. Arrival of Cindy, however, cut LuAnn's territory in half with predictable consequences. And when Rebecca came along, dropping each share to one-third, the fight was on.

No pompous potentate ever guarded territorial boundaries with greater intensity. LuAnn had the right side, Cindy the left and Rebecca the center. Poor Rebecca. The center isn't always a nice place to be. Seat padding is thin and no matter how hard you try, you can't keep your feet from sliding down one side or the other of the hump on the floor.

If I live to be a hundred I'll never forget the muffled sound of "oofs" echoing from the outback. We knew what it meant. Rebecca had gotten it again—strayed across someone's line and paid the price for her folly.

It was always the same. I'd look up and there in the rear-view mirror would be the angelic face of LuAnn batting her innocent, blue eyes and smiling beneficently. I never once caught her digging her elbow into Rebecca's ribs, although I suspect Rebecca never realized until she reached adulthood that ribs aren't supposed to ache.

Not that she couldn't defend herself. Rebecca used her long, skinny fingers and sharp nails to patrol the central sector. She knew full well how to use them and she never bothered to feign innocence.

Cindy, on the other hand, was the quiet type. She could and did dish out punishment when her territory came under attack, but most of the time she just slept. She had an innate distrust of alien bathrooms, particularly the outhouse at her grandparents' farm. She never went there if she could avoid it. Because of this her disposition deteriorated at an accelerating rate with passage of time. By the close of a three-day weekend she was about as sociable as a junk-yard dog with mange.

Then Fred was born. There was no way we were going to consign him to that aboriginal jungle we called the outback while he was still a baby. For his own protection his place was between Mrs. H and me. At first he lay on a blanket. As soon as he learned to sit he graduated to the peach crate.

The peach crate was exactly what its name indicates—a peach crate modified slightly by the addition of a center brace and a padded cover. That faithful old peach crate served each of the kids as both a raised platform at the dining room table and an elevated perch from which to see out the car windows.

Fred was all over both it and me, usually driving the little rock he imagined was a bus. Across my shoulder, up my neck, across my forehead, down the other side and back again. It went on by the hour.

My right arm became the first workable retractable automobile safety belt for children. With it I saved him from more than one nasty bump. Now, of course, he's so stubborn he won't even use the seat belt in his sports car.

Eventually though, he too had to leave for the outback. We bought a station wagon and assigned him space on the floor behind the back seat—far enough back so we could scarcely hear the sounds of combat.

It's different today. Coming back from Iowa City, Mrs. H and I reversed driving assignments. We even tuned to a different radio station just for the sake of variety. She got some knitting done and I read the newspaper. Not once in the eight hours did I find myself reaching back to discipline anyone, nor did Mrs. H find it necessary to threaten dire consequences.

We drank coffee and talked about this and that—whatever happened to the peach crate, how LuAnn managed to fight so dirty and look so innocent, how Rebecca managed to survive all those years surrounded by hostile forces, how Cindy grew up so healthy with such an irregular childhood, whatever happened to the rock that looked like a bus, and a dozen and one other memories of other days and other travels.

It was a thoroughly boring trip--and we loved every peaceful, languid, tranquil minute of it.

Lew Hudson

Zip: Mrs. H Zapped Mr. H

Never before have I heard such cacophony. It started innocently enough as a game of Zip. Zip, as many of you will recall, is that game families have used for years to keep the kids busy while traveling.

Rules vary, but the way I learned it a white horse was worth one point, a white mule, five points and a cemetery 10. There were only two ways to wind—either be ahead on points when you drove into the driveway or zip an old man riding a bicycle with white whiskers outside the city limits.

And that rarely happened. I saw one only once. I was on a train and saw him out the window at a crossing. I zipped him loudly. You have to zip out loud or it doesn't count. The other people thought I was nuts.

Afterward, no one in the family would believe me. "You? You actually saw an old man riding a bicycle with white whiskers outside the city limits? Naw, you're just pulling our leg."

Only I wasn't. I really did see one.

There are rules variations. One branch of the family says you lose all your points every time you cross the Mississippi River.

Another says that's not true, but a white cow mistakenly zipped as a horse draws a 10-point demerit. And if you zip a white pig by mistake, you're out of the game for 100 miles.

But Sunday, en route home from a family wedding in Iowa, we weren't arguing over rules. Mrs. H, our son Fred, our daughter Cindy, and I knew them backward and forward.

We started a game in the vicinity of Ottumwa and before we'd gone 30 miles the fight was on. First, Fred tricked me into falsely zipping a white cow. "You're ten points in the hole," he chortled.

I countered by staring intently toward a grove of distant evergreens that could have, but didn't, enclose a cemetery. He didn't bite.

Mrs. H zipped a white horse standing broadside near a barn. Cindy's zip sounded like an echo.

"I was first," Mrs. H said. "Yours doesn't count."

"It does too," she squealed. "There were two of them."

"How come I didn't see but one?" Mrs. H asked.

"It was facing the other direction."

"It can't be a legal zip," Fred said, "unless someone else sees it too."

"Can too," she shouted.

If it hadn't been for the next cemetery, I shudder to think what might have happened, but about that time Mrs. H yelled a cemetery zip.

"What do you mean, 'zip'?" Fred said. "All that was showing was the top of some cemetery trees."

"I saw tombstones," she stoutly maintained. Then it was Cindy's turn to call foul. "I didn't see any cemetery," she said. "More than one has to see it for it to count."

"When you're my age you can do anything you want," Mrs. H said.

I kept quiet. I remembered a country cemetery a little further up the road, way back from the road from the highway. Sort of behind a hill and not anywhere close to a town. Even with the Memorial Day flags to mark it, I figured this one was mine.

About a mile before it was to come into view, I saw Mrs. H start looking over my way. Then she started leaning forward in her seat.

Not so as to be noticeable, you understand—just a slow shift forward.

This was getting serious. I knew that she knew that I knew there was a cemetery that would soon come into view. She kept talking to allay suspicion. I stretched a little to distract her. "I'm getting a leg cramp," I said. "Maybe it would help if I moved the seat forward a little."

Good try Hudson. She leaned even farther forward. This was going to be a matter of reaction time—hers against mine. The hill hiding the cemetery came alongside and started to slide by. I was looking left. So was she. Who would see it first? Victory hung in the balance.

And then it happened. A smelly old Dodge pulled out to pass. Out of the corner of my eye I spotted a bunch of kids in the back. Heads were bobbing up and down as they pounded away at each other. The woman in the front seat was turned half-way around, flailing away indiscriminately.

It was a great show, and I glanced toward it. Just for a split-second, mind you, but that was enough.

"Zip," she said with a shout.

Now, I ask you, where are all those old men riding bicycles with white whiskers outside the city limits when you need them?

Lew Hudson

The Father of the Bride Isn't in Spotlight

Everyone in the church is looking in his direction but every eye is on the woman at his side.

It's like singing the national anthem at a football game—everyone stands respectfully, but it's the game, not the anthem that is on their minds.

Even his daughter looks beyond him. As much as she has loved her father and as important as he has been in her life, another man has become paramount. Fortunately there is no limit to love. A daughter does not have to cast a father aside to make room for a husband.

These and other thoughts raced through my mind last week as I stood at the rear of the church waiting for the organist to signal the longest walk a father can make. The radiant woman now holding my arm used to be in my arms. She loved for me to dance with her to the music of her favorite song, "Wake Up Little Susie."

Her least favorite was "Old McDonald Had a Farm." It's dreadful monotony always put her to sleep. Every time I'd start to sing it she'd say, "No, no Daddy."

In high school she had a Volkswagen Beetle—the only car I could afford to give her. To keep it running I bought a book and became a VW mechanic. She was my helper.

Today all of the grease is gone from beneath her fingernails and the dirt smudges from her face. Every hair is in place. She is beautiful.

Standing at the back of the church there is nothing a father can say that makes any sense at all. The years have come and gone. All the advice has been given. All the lessons have been learned.

You want to tell her how much she is loved, but she already knows that. You want to tell her how proud you are, but she already knows that. You want to tell her she will always have a special place in your heart, but she already knows that.

So you don't say anything. It's just as well. Say what's really on your mind and you'll both break out in tears and that's no way for a bride to come down the aisle.

So you stand there with her arm in yours. You look down the aisle to the pastor, the attendants and the waiting groom—the man who will from this point on be the focal point in her life.

Out of the corner of your eye you catch her looking up at you. Daddy's little girl is all grown up. And every eye is on her.

These Boots Were Made for Wearing

Even in a world of constant change, some things seem to go on forever. At least, that was the lament of our daughters when they were growing up. In support of their argument, they cited Plaintiffs' Exhibit No. 1—a pair of yellow plastic boots--and Plaintiffs' Exhibit No. 2—the peach-colored dotted Swiss nylon dress.

Old family pictures seem to bear out their contention. New clothes every season were financially impossible around our house in those years. Make-do and hand-me-downs were the rule. The fact that our first three children were girls helped considerably.

The famed yellow boots, purchased first for our oldest daughter, LuAnn, when she was in second grade, turned out to be practically immortal. We were looking at some old pictures a while back and the yellow boots showed up year after year.

They were truly remarkable. Capable, it seemed, of growing with the feet they protected. In fact, they actually grew even faster. When we bought the boots, we naturally picked one size too large in order to get more wear out of them. But as it turned out, they were still an inch too long when LuAnn quit wearing them years later.

LuAnn swore that, had she not put her foot down, so to speak, she would still have been wearing those boots at her high school prom. As it was, she willed them to her sister, Cindy, when her feet got big enough to almost fill them. That was about in fifth grade, as I recall.

Cindy, in turn, presented them to her sister, Rebecca, along about seventh grade when Rebecca's feet got large enough to practically fill them. No wet-weather family picture over a dozen years failed to include those yellow boots on someone's feet.

The tradition stopped of course with Fred. He wouldn't hear of wearing them. Didn't even want to talk about it. Tennies were good enough for school, thank you, and that's all there was to it.

I argued the case, pointing out that the yellow boots were gender-generic and still perfectly good. "There's a lot of wear left in them," I said hopefully, but he wasn't buying. Instead I was. I had to shell out 30 bucks for a pair of insulated snowmobile boots for his outdoor activities.

I can't remember how we finally got rid of the yellow things, but I think Mrs. H unloaded them on some other young family at one of her famous garage sales. For all I know, they're still serving a family of youngsters somewhere. Perhaps still growing, too.

The peach colored dotted Swiss nylon dress was a similar phenomenon. Again it was bought new for LuAnn. She, being the oldest, always got first crack at the female clothing.

It was originally an Easter dress. Although it was a trifle large the first year, LuAnn grew into it in time—and eventually out of it, but not soon enough to satisfy her. As I recall, she wore it for special occasions for two or three years—or maybe it was four or five, as she claimed. Time has a way of getting away from a person.

Then the dress went to Cindy for another two or three years. To hear her tell it, of course, it was more like a lifetime. Then it went to Rebecca for another three or four years. And when she was done with it, the ruffles were just as stiff, the skirt just as swishy and the sleeves just as puffy as they were when it was new. In fact, you could hardly tell the dress had ever been worn.

The pictures, though, say otherwise. Every Sunday-go-to-meeting picture for a dozen years in our albums has someone wearing that dress. But at least Mrs. H and I had the common decency not to require anyone to wear the yellow boots and the peach dress at the same time. The dress too, was finally disposed of via a garage sale.

If I were a betting man I would wager that a survey of the churches in Worthington this Easter Sunday would reveal a little girl dressed in a peach colored, dotted Swiss nylon party dress.

It will look as good as new, and the girl wearing it will hate it.

Lew Hudson

Uncles Can Provide Special Kind of Parenting

Every kid needs an Uncle Les. That doesn't have to be his name. It could as well be Willy, Joe, Sam, Bob or Charlie. The name isn't important. The role is. Uncles are a kid's best friend.

Uncles don't have to put on a pretense like fathers. Discipline isn't their job. Images aren't important. Uncles can just have fun and enjoy kids.

Uncles can regale kids with stories their fathers would just as soon forget—stories that puncture parental pomposity and expose the human side fathers think they have to hide.

Uncle Les was my father's younger brother. He knew Dad before he got so serious about life. He wanted us to know our father that way too. Through him we learned of Dad's boastful claim at the age of 16 that he knew how to drive a car when in fact he didn't and ended up laying a Model-T Ford on its side.

Through Les we learned that Dad once got a speeding ticket on a date with Mom. We learned a lot from him. Dad's past was never safe when Les was around. He loved to make him squirm. Les didn't have any kids of his own. Maybe that's why we loved him so much.

He figured it was an uncle's duty to spoil his nephews and nieces. When Les was around the rules were a little looser and the laughs a little louder. It was Les who organized a fly swatting meet one hot August afternoon when the flies were bothering his afternoon nap. "I'll pay a penny a dozen," he proclaimed.

He figured we'd thin out the swarm in the house, but since he didn't say so we went on a foray to the outhouse and nearly broke him up in business. Les was always dreaming up odd ball things like that to delight kids.

He could even laugh when the joke was on him. One summer he showed up for our annual fishing vacation with a brand new steel casting rod. It was so flexible and strong, he boasted, that it could be bent from tip to butt without breaking or kinking. "Here, I'll show you," he said. It snapped into three pieces. Les laughed louder than anyone.

That's the way he was. He kept things in perspective. His life was an example of that. He even showed us how to die. He was fishing off the coast of California with his wife of more than 50 years when he hooked, fought and landed a trophy salmon.

While acknowledging the congratulations of others on board, he suffered a heart attack and died. Every kid needs an Uncle Les.

An Older Brother's Wise Advice

Every kid should have an older brother like mine. Four years older and infinitely smarter, Dick was what you might call an inspiration. Those of us in the family who were younger looked up to him for leadership. He never failed us.

Not that his advice was always good because it wasn't. It was just that he, like any good leader, was convinced it was good. That's all it took.

Dick wasn't much of a physical specimen—asthma saw to that—but he made up for it in an intellectual way. He had an inquiring mind full of ideas needing to be tested. It was he who answered a magazine advertisement from Mandrake the Magician and received a small wooden vase which could be manipulated so as to make a little ball within it appear and disappear. It was the mainstay of several neighborhood magic shows he produced and directed. No one in the neighborhood ever figured it out.

He played in the band and, when the occasion presented itself, talked me into entering into an unproductive two-year relationship with an oboe. He had a newspaper route and hired me as his assistant for 15 cents per week. It was my first job. He took a summer job working on a golf course. The following spring he talked his boss into letting me take over the position.

He was always doing things like that. The summer after my first year in college he suggested we go to Detroit and get jobs in an auto plant. He said we'd make a lot of money. That sounded good. Unfortunately it wasn't. Auto companies that summer weren't hiring college kids. We stuck it out as long as our money lasted and headed home.

The trip, though, taught me a valuable lesson in what assertive self-confidence can do. En route to Detroit we were riding a New York Central passenger train—not the 20th Century Limited—but still one of the line's finer trains. It rolled out of Chicago about 8 p.m.

Naturally, we were traveling coach fare. A few miles out of Chicago we decided to play some chess, but try as we might we couldn't balance the chess-board on our knees.

"Let's go back to the club car," Dick said. "We can find a table there." Not one to argue with a man of such revered wisdom and advanced years (he was 23 at the time) I agreed. Before he opened the door he said, "Now we'll just walk in as if we belonged and no one will say anything."

We did and they didn't. We found a couple of overstuffed chairs, pulled them up to a lamp table, set up the chessboard and started our game. Other passengers, most of who seemed to be banker and lawyer types, watched with bemused interest. Two or three asked for explanation of the various moves the game entailed. We happily obliged.

For nearly three hours we played. After 10 p.m. the kibitzers one by one started putting out their cigars and heading off to the Pullman compartments. Finally about 11 p.m. the conductor, who had been quietly doing his paper work on another table toward the rear of the car, ambled over to our table and said with a twinkle in his eye, "I expect you fellows should head back to your coach now."

We hadn't fooled him a bit. He knew all along we didn't belong in the club car. I suppose most of the bankers and lawyers knew it too, but for so long as we acted like we belonged they accepted us.

I wonder how people who don't have older brothers learn that basic rule of life.

The Truth Behind the Great Dogfight

How can I say this? Duty compels me to report the truth, yet if I do, I will impugn my own brother's integrity. It's a job I don't relish but he's been telling the story wrong for almost 50 years. Someone has to set the record straight. People have a right to know the truth about one of the greatest aerial dogfights of World War II.

I know. I was there. So was he, so he doesn't have any excuse for telling it wrong. You'll need a little background. When we were growing up, Hawkeye Bob and I shared a bedroom. We also shared a love for making model airplanes.

Our room was a model airplane museum. The ceiling was covered with models suspended on threads in realistic flying position. Each was made from bits of balsa wood glued together and covered with tissue paper. Power was supplied by rubber bands stretched from nose to tail.

The best I ever built was a Boeing P-12, an open-cockpit biplane fighter of the 1930s. It was a veteran of dozens of flights, some off the roof of our front porch.

Bob's best was a Stinson Gull Wing, a popular cabin monoplane of that era. Being new, it hadn't been flown as much but it was pretty stable and performed nicely.

For almost 50 years the argument over what started the dogfight has raged between the two of us. Now the second generation has taken it up. At family gatherings his offspring have one version. Mine have another. Mine, of course, have only half the truth. It was about 7 p.m., winter and dark. We were in our room studying. At least I was.

But instead of studying from a book, Hawkeye Bob was studying aeronautics—using my Boeing P-12. Before I realized what was happening, he undertook to test the structural integrity of its landing gear by subjecting it to a violent forced landing.

He denies that, of course. He maintains he was just admiring how nicely it glided and never had the slightest idea that the left landing gear would be wiped out when it smashed against the top of the dresser.

As you might expect, this did not sit well with me. I was trying diligently to do my homework while my own brother was deliberately crashing my best model airplane. Now, I didn't assault him—although no jury in the country would have convicted me, considering the provocation. Instead I plucked down his Stinson and conducted an experiment of my own to see if a Stinson Gull wing could go supersonic. It couldn't. The right wing flew off just before it crashed into the wall.

And that's when the fight started. We squared off, swapping blows and accusations. The noise was horrendous. So horrendous, in fact, that we didn't hear approaching footsteps.

You've heard of the footsteps of doom? That's what these were. It was our mother, demanding to know what in tarnation was going on.

"He broke my airplane," I said.
"He broke my airplane," Bob said.

Quicker than it takes to tell it, our mother, seeing both planes on the floor, stamped them into kindling.

"There," she said, "I broke both airplanes." And downstairs she went. It got mighty quiet. Bob looked at me. I looked at him.

He lovingly scooped up the pieces of his Stinson. I affectionately gathered my P-12. We consigned them to the same wastebasket. I can't say that the experience made us any wiser but I like to think it taught us the value of conciliation.

Before third-party intervention, the landing gear of my P-12 could have been repaired. So could the wing of his Stinson. Afterward they were destroyed.

And that's the story. To this day, Hawkeye Bob maintains the crash was an accident—that he was innocently gliding my airplane. Which, of course, is poppycock

I don't make any bones about the last flight of his Stinson. That was sheer anger at work. I just wish he'd be as honest and tell his kids the truth.

Lew Hudson

She Was Dead—It Was One of Those Things

She was dead and no one could understand why. The minister at the funeral tried to explain it. He couldn't. He read the chapter in Proverbs about the value of a good wife and it only made the loss more intense.

The grandfather of her two children tried, but emotion overcame him. Stunned townspeople tried but the best they could do was, "just one of those things."

It was just one of those things. Every day she rode with her husband to her job in a neighboring town and every day he drove on to the city where he worked in a major hospital. This day was no different. He stopped to pick her up in the evening. They were talking about the day's experiences as their car picked up speed heading out of town.

And then it was there—an onrushing station wagon suddenly veering over the center line directly into her path.

There was no escape. The cars slammed together. She never had a chance.

She lay there pinned in the wreckage, mortally injured. He lay there beside her, conscious, but seriously injured. Ambulance and rescue crews from three towns raced to the scene. One was the Pleasantville crew of which he was one of the veteran paramedic members. They had to cut and pry the car apart for 15 minutes to get them out. "Help her first," he said. "She's hurt worse than me."

A few feet away the other driver lay in the wreckage of his car, critically injured and unconscious. It was just one of those things.

Just one of those things happens almost every day. Last year 626 persons died in Iowa traffic accidents. They're called accidents but all of them aren't. Last year 251 persons died in Iowa crashes in which the driving ability of one or more of the drivers was impaired by alcohol. That is not accidental.

Mark this as one of those. Authorities said the driver of the other car was a patient at a mental hospital. He was free to leave the hospital grounds but he was not authorized to drive and certainly not to drink, yet he did both. CB radios had been crackling back up the road talking about the driver who was all over the highway. "He ran me off the road." "Me too," they said. The state patrol had been notified but they got to him only after he had crossed the center line and killed an innocent woman.

The church was not large enough to hold everyone. The community was stunned. Everyone loved Rena. She was the first to show up with a hot dish when someone was ill or when there was to be a lunch after a funeral. At family gatherings she was always up to her elbows in dishwater because "someone has to do them." She made quilts and did ceramics. She loved to cook. She adored her children. Her personality was as beautiful as her face and both were striking.

Now she lay dead in a closed casket surrounded by flowers recalling the beauty that had been hers. Her friends were there. Her family was there. Her seven-year old daughter and her 10-year old son were there.

The only one absent was her husband. He lay in a hospital bed with tubes and needles and bandages and pain. And the minister struggled to find words to explain why it happened. Finding none he could only quote Rena's seven-year-old daughter who said in her childish innocence, "Maybe God needed Mommy to bake for the angels."

No one talked about the real reason—that there is a drug called alcohol and that one of its qualities is to dull the senses and impair muscular coordination, and that people consume it willingly and in quantities sufficient to destroy their judgment, and that society is unwilling and unable to adequately control the drug's availability.

To such a problem there seem to be no really good answers, and so this time it was Pleasantville's turn for "just one of those things." Tomorrow it will be another town and family and the day after that another….and another…and another.

But don't blame God for it.

Lew Hudson

Gawks Perfect for Squirmers

One of the sacred responsibilities of grandparents is to pass on time-tested ways of keeping kids quiet in church. Parental instincts are clearly inadequate and trial and error takes too long. Considering the penalty for misbehaving, some kids don't have that much fun.

Particularly preacher's kids—PKs.

I was one. We grew up silent and scared. Punishment was swift and severe for even the slightest commotion in church. I still feel sorry for my brother Bob who got into a scuffle with a friend midway through the sermon one Sunday morning.

Dad stopped and admonished Bob to settle down. Bob later contended the guy grabbed something that belonged to him and he was just trying to get it back, but that defense didn't have a chance. His goose was cooked.

Sentence was executed promptly after church and Bob had trouble settling down with any degree of comfort for about three days. Only old folks sleep through sermons. Children are stimulated by them and hell fire and brimstone warnings don't work.

More creative ways are needed to help keep the restless ones occupied. Coloring in the letters on the bulletin with a pencil is a good place to start, but it won't satisfy very long. Tic-tac-toe works if you can repress the victory cries. A chronograph wristwatch with its stop and go button is useful. A pocket watch that ticks also fascinates.

There's a way of folding and rolling a handkerchief to form a reasonable imitation of a mouse. Folded another way it can become a miniature hammock. Paper boats are nice. Usually, though, by the time preachers get to their thirdlies, ordinary diversions are wearing thin.

Then comes gawk time.

Gawks are wonderful. No child can resist them. Gawks get even the whiniest children safely through the sermon wrap-up. Here's how to make one.

Start with a square piece of paper. The bulletin is OK even though it's printed on 8 ½ by 11-inch paper. To get a square all you have to do is fold one edge diagonally down to the other and tear off the surplus. Once that's done fold it the other way to mark the center.

Then fold three corners to the center. Turn the paper over and fold the fourth to the center on that side. Turn it back to the first side and fold all four corners to the original center. Voila! You have created a gawk.

Draw whatever you want in the way of eyes, hair and nostrils on the front, fluff it out and let the fun begin.

And if the preacher unexpectedly goes into a fourthly just keep on making gawks in various sizes because there's nothing big gawks love to do more than eat little gawks.

Heirloom Meets Tragic Demise

We had an accident out at the Hudson house the other day. Son Fred inadvertently knocked over and shattered a genuine, handmade, one-of-a-kind ceramic pencil holder. It was an heirloom that had been in our family for almost half a generation.

Fashioned from clay, it had been carefully molded by hand into the approximate shape of a soft drink can, decorated with numerous blobs of partially rounded lumps of clay, painted an unusual shade of chartreuse and carefully fired in a kiln to preserve it forever. It was even signed on the bottom by the artist.

The pencil holder had occupied a place of honor next to the lamp on Mrs. H's writing desk ever since the day Fred finished it as a school art project and proudly brought it home.

Fred, naturally, felt just terrible about breaking it. "I picked up the lamp," he said, "and it fell on the floor."

Trying desperately to control my emotions, I said it was sure a doggone shame but those things happen once in a while.

Mrs. H was equally hard pressed to conceal her true feelings as she commiserated with him, saying it had been there on the desk so long she had almost become used to its unique color and unusual shape. Both did have a way of growing on you.

In some ways the pencil holder reminded me of the ashtray one of our daughters made for me as a Brownie Scout project. Also fashioned by hand, it was made of brownish-red clay she personally excavated down by the lake.

In all honesty, just having that ashtray around the house contributed to my decision to quit smoking.

These sorts of objects go along with being a parent. Take my desk at the office, for example. On it I have the nicest pair of pretty rock paperweights you'd ever want to see. One is painted black with irregular gold splotches and the other silver with abstract flower designs. I don't remember which of the kids made which—it's been so long—but my desk wouldn't look natural without them.

I keep them in the cardboard pencil holder that was a Christmas present from Rebecca in 1968 or 1969. Right next to it is my Valentine's Day 1972 smile face miniature trophy. More than once, on tough days, I have looked at the grinning yellow face and heeded the admonition printed on its base. "Keep smiling," it says.

Mrs. H has a box full of similar items on a shelf in the closet. We look at them every time we decide to move. That's been twice in the last 25 years.

After last week's catastrophe, Fred picked up the pieces but the chartreuse pencil holder was a mess. All that was left were three or four major chunks and a handful of chips. "I could try and glue it back together, Dad," he said.

"No," I replied. "I'm afraid it's too far gone. I hate to say it, but I think we'll just have to throw it away."

Mrs. H didn't say anything but I could tell from the look in her eye she agreed with me. I remember seeing that same look the day Fred announced he was going to get rid of his beer can collection.

CHAPTER 3

Hudson's Theorem

Dad's philosophical views on life have always been unique and straightforward. His thirst for knowledge and the pursuit of the elusive answers to life's most persistent mysteries have driven the seasoned writer throughout his long career. Perhaps the greatest legacy he can give to his children is his impeccable honor and the knowledge to strive to take the right path in our lives. The best advice he ever gave us: "You have the strength within yourself to do whatever you need to do. Make your decision and never look back."

Lew Hudson

Behold Hudson's Theorem

It takes a lot of pondering for a columnist to stay ahead of the calendar. I like to be about a week ahead because once in a while I just can't ponder worth a hoot. I ponder while driving, while walking down the street, during television commercials, while Mrs. H is talking and sometimes in church—when it is apparent the preacher didn't do enough pondering.

The other day I was pondering in the shower. Normally I don't do that. Shower-pondering isn't very productive. There usually isn't time, at least not on weekday mornings. Weekends, though are different. There is time for the brain to get organized, which is what pondering is all about.

This happened on a weekend. As I was soaping up my right arm, I noticed an old scar there. It's one I picked up while building a garage 20 years ago. A nail sticking out of a falling board was to blame. I don't suppose I'd looked at that scar in the last five years. There hasn't been any reason to. It hasn't changed. It never does.

But looking at it reminded me what a satisfying task building that garage had been. I designed and built it myself and, if I do say so, it was as close to being straight and true the day I sold it as it was the day I finished it—which of course isn't saying much.

That got me to pondering about that time a great truth dawned on me. I think I'll call it Hudson's Theorem. It'll make me just as famous as that fellow Murphy, who propounded the law that bears his name.

Hudson's Theorem goes like this: The memory of how a scar was inflicted is as permanent as the scar itself. My, but that is profound. I wonder why I never thought of it before. I turned my right arm over and sure enough, memories of how I got the four scars between my elbow and wrist flooded back. I was 14 and jerking sodas at Welch's Drug Store in Bloomfield, Iowa. We ran out of milk one rainy summer afternoon so I grabbed a bottle and ran to the grocery, four doors down the street. On the way I slipped and fell, the bottle shattered and I slid across it on my elbow.

Inspired now I started looking for other evidences of a long, hard life to see what they might conjure up. Over on the left elbow I spotted the small scar I picked up one evening at a Boy Scout meeting when Howard Martin came up to me and whacked me on the elbow with his face. Poor Howard broke his glasses. Served him right though. I figured if he was brazen enough to batter my elbow with his face it wasn't my responsibility to chip in on a new pair of glasses.

Right next to it I saw that tattoo that has been with me since fourth grade. Bob Chadwick did it when he jabbed me with a lead pencil. The neat scar on my abdomen is a lasting memento of Dr. Paul Laube of Dubuque, Iowa, who in his role as a church layman, first convinced me I should become a Presbyterian and then, a month later, cashed in when my appendix flared up. I'll never forget the five days I spent in the hospital because would you believe it, they had the gall to charge me $8 a day for a room.

On my left knee is the record of how I flunked a Boy Scout cooking merit badge and on the same day earned one for first aid. While working on the cooking badge, I was cutting shavings with which to start a fire. The hunting knife slipped. That ended the cooking test but I seized the opportunity to work on my first aid badge. An emergency bandage slowed the leakage enough so my buddy could haul me on a bicycle to Doc Gilfillan's office. Instead of stitching the cut Doc used some experimental metal clips someone had invented to close it up. They didn't work very well because the scars that the clips themselves inflicted still line both sides of the knife scar.

One of my more memorable scars is on the back of my left hand. It's a leftover from the time I was treated by a veterinarian for a gash inflicted by a racing turkey.

I was down in Cuero, Texas to take part in the Great Gobbler Gallop turkey race between Texas and Minnesota. While I was attempting to corral the Minnesota bird (a wild gobbler named Paycheck) so Dr. Charlie Tubbs could give it a shot of penicillin, the bird got me with a claw. Doc Charlie gave Paycheck the needle and me a generous swabbing with antiseptic so I guess it came out about even.

One scar on my back and another on my left ear are the two happiest scars of my life, because they remind me that I am a living breathing, two-time cancer winner. That in turn, reminded me to remind you that doctors can usually cure cancer if they get at it soon enough.

About that time I started to run out of hot water. Besides, I figured I'd pondered about long enough to write a column. You just read the result.

Lew Hudson

Writer's Block is a Terrifying Dream

Nightmares come in many shapes and sizes. Kids see vicious monsters and terrifying apparitions. Teen-agers have a different set of bugaboos—dreams of personal rejection, embarrassment and faux pas.

Young parents have nightmares of economic failure, premature death and family tragedy. Older people dream of losing their jobs or becoming disabled.

One type of nightmare gives way to another as years go by. Some are universal. One is the fear of falling. Most people dream of falling off a high building or cliff.

Tradition says if you hit the ground you'll never wake up but I don't know how anyone determined that. Other nightmarish dreams are common to most people—being caught naked in public, running for your life but making no progress, reaching in vain for something.

Psychologists and psychiatrists are divided on the significance of dreams. Me, I have my own special nightmare. It's recurrent. I've dreamed it for years. It's always the same.

Well, almost always. One facet has changed. In the old days I would see myself seated at my typewriter. Nowadays I'm at a word-processing terminal. The dream, however, is the same.

I'm facing deadline. Nothing is going right. The phone rings, but no one is there. I pick up the phone book and drop it on the floor. I type, but the words are garbled. My chair is too low. I try to raise it but can't. I look for my notes. They've disappeared. I search my desk. They aren't there. I wrack my brain but can remember only scattered bits of information.

The clock speeds toward deadline. The harder I try the more slowly I go. The more I concentrate the less I accomplish. My strength drains away. I grow wearier. The story I am trying to write is impossible to complete.

Words that normally flow are clogged in my brain. What does appear on the screen makes no sense. I clear the screen and try again. It only gets worse.

I concentrate. I struggle. I think. I type. Time flies. My fingers crawl. My mind stagnates. My brow is sweaty. My eyes hurt. My head aches.

And finally I can go no further. All my experience is for naught. I am stalled. My nightmare always ends the same way. I am at deadline. The story is missing only one line—the line that will tie it together, transform a mundane story into a masterpiece. I know what it should say. I've known it all along. A writer always knows what the last line will say before the first is written.

But in the waning moments of my recurrent nightmare I am paralyzed...unable...no matter how hard I try...to write...another...

It's the Church That's Lost

It's a family tradition. Hudsons don't ask for directions. My Dad was like that. So was his Dad. I see traces of it in our son.

Mrs. H despairs. I keep on going.

A couple weeks ago I was driving from our motel to the church in Columbia, Missouri, for our daughter's wedding. I knew where the church was—somewhere between the downtown area and the University of Missouri.

The problem was the freeway. By the time I found a way to get across it I was in an unfamiliar part of town and the compass in my car suddenly malfunctioned.

To make it worse, behind me were two carloads of family members depending on me to lead them on. "You're lost," Mrs. H said. "Why don't you stop and ask for directions."

"I know where I am," I replied. "It's the church that's lost."

Then I saw College Street. That, I figured, should go directly to the university which should put me close to the church. Except, soon learned, it went to Stephens College. "Oh, oh," I said to myself. Hudsons don't panic. Hudsons forge ahead. Or turn back.

Quick as a flash I flipped on the turn signals, went into a side street, wheeled around the circular drive of a sorority house and headed back toward town with the relatives in tow.

By this time there were a number of suggestions coming from the right side of the car, but I focused my attention on picking a likely street heading toward the university. At the first intersection nothing looked familiar.

On to the next. Same thing. Then the third. There it was.

I hung a right, wheeled into the church parking lot and got out. "Here we are," I said with a smile.

The relatives said it seemed to them we went a little out of our way, but I said I wanted to show them that beautiful sorority house. I couldn't quite hear what Mrs. H was saying but later she vowed to add this excursion to my list. She ranked it right between our midnight honeymoon tour of back streets in West Liberty, Iowa, and the scenic tour of Waterloo, Iowa, a few years back.

Waterloo is one of her favorites. She contended I was lost. I said I knew where I was—somewhere south of Highway 20 and east of Highway 63.

She said looking for that shortcut was dumb. I said it was a good chance to see what a nice city Waterloo was. Driving past one house I looked in a lighted window and noticed a family enjoying supper. "Look," I said. "They're just finishing eating."

"They were saying grace the last time we drove by," she muttered.

Daniel Boone used to say he was never lost although one time he was confused for about three days.

I wonder if his grandmother was a Hudson.

L.A.H. Could Become a Rich Man Any Day Now

It's only a matter of time until I become a multimillionaire. It says so in the letter I got the other day.

$5 million, It said. That has a nice ring to it--$167,000 a year for 30 years. Ordinarily I'd be a little suspicious, but the address on this letter included my middle initial. I haven't used that since I was in high school.

That must mean something. It's pretty obvious they've done more than a little checking before deciding to give the money to me. Otherwise they wouldn't give two whoops about my middle name.

The letter said I sailed through the first round without any problem. Not everyone is so lucky, it said. Even fewer, it continued, make it through Round Two of the selection process. Would you believe I did that too?

That must have been when they looked up my middle name. I'll bet only those whose middle names begin with an "A" made the second cut. When I pointed that out to Mrs. H she laughed.

I told her he who laughs last laughs best. "Your middle name starts with an 'M,'" I said, "and I don't see you getting a letter."

That quieted her down.

The letter said only 4 percent of the people get through to the championship round and I'm one of them.

"They've already made out my certificate," I said to Mrs. H. "See here? There's my name—Lew A. Hudson—and my address. And it says down here at the bottom that I will be notified by a special courier who will drive up to our house in a stretch limousine. Boy, are you going to eat your words."

She's a born skeptic. "It says you'll be notified by special courier if you are a winner," she said, "not when."

"That's just a technicality," I said. "It's pretty obvious they've already made up their mind. Why else would they issue me a special 22-digit identification number? And why did they put my initials in the middle of that red star on my certificate?"

"That doesn't mean a thing," she said. "Someone's always running one of those sweepstakes. Your chances are virtually nil."

That can't be true, I said. If it was, the Reader's Digest would have long since done an expose. The Reader's Digest, I said, is the nation's moral arbiter. It exposes crime and corruption. It extols virtuous conduct and heroic deeds. It crusades against communism, socialism, plagiarism and, welfarism. It exposes judges who don't judge, teachers who don't teach, lawmakers who don't legislate, welfare systems that don't work, governments that don't govern and leaders who mislead.

"As long as the Reader's Digest is out there watching," I said, "no one would dare mislead people into thinking they were going to win $5 million."

"Did you notice who sent you that letter?" she said.

Summer Research Work Flies By

"A flea and a fly in a flue were imprisoned so what should they do? Said the flea, let us fly, said the fly let us flee, so they flew through the flaw in the flue."

That old rhyme came to mind the other day in connection with some scientific research I was doing out on the patio. For those of you who aren't scientifically inclined, patio research is done by settling into a comfortable chair, elevating the feet into a second chair, leaning the head back and closing the eyes half way to appear asleep. That way the things you are researching are less likely to be aware they are under scrutiny.

It was a warm day, ideal for my scientific project—behavioral patterns of the common house fly. Well, actually two flies. They were resting on the table. One was a big old house fly, the other a little old house fly—kind of scrawny, actually.

But there was more to it than that. The big old house fly was not only larger but more colorful—wings more lustrous, eyes a reddish brown, hairy body almost black.

By contrast, the little old house fly was about half as big, eyes a dirty brown and body a faded gray.

And they held their wings different. The big guy held his at about a 45-degree angle from his body. The little guy folded his one on top of the other over the center of his back. Both had built-in soda straw mouths to suck up tidbits of whatever it is that flies enjoy, although the little guy looked like pickings had been pretty slim lately.

And neither cared which way the wind was blowing. That surprised me. Most creatures pay attention to the wind. Birds perch with their heads into it to facilitate taking off. But even though they were aerodynamic creatures these two house flies ignored it.

One was facing crosswind and the other directly downwind. I eased my hand up to each in turn and watched carefully as they took off. Both leaped into the air without taking so much as a single step to turn into the wind.

Now before you write an irate letter suggesting I get an honest job, let me say that the pursuit of scientific knowledge requires patient observation. That's something I've tried for years to explain to Mrs. H. She thinks when I'm outside I should be mowing the yard, watering the flowers or digging dandelions. It's getting so I sometimes don't even bother to tell her my scientific discoveries.

You readers, of course, are different. You appreciate these things. How many of you knew before you read this that there are two distinctly different kinds of house flies? Or that flies can take off downwind? Or that flies fold their wings in different ways? Neither did I.

Just stop and think. We may be the only persons in the whole world who know. And it's all because I generously agreed to donate one of my valuable afternoons to research. It's a tough job but somebody has to do it.

Case of the Missing Napkin

Mrs. H has this thing about sticky fingers. It's a male problem. Men are always getting their fingers in the food and looking around for something to wipe them on.

Women don't. Food doesn't seem to stick to them. Mrs. H can pare apples, make pie crust, put together an apple pie and finish with nothing more than a smidgen of flour on her hands.

Men can't. When a man picks up a slice of bread and peanut butter about a third of it ends up on his fingers. When a man eats fried chicken the grease runs down to his wrists. When a man picks up a pickle the ends of his fingers are preserved in vinegar.

The natural instinct is to wipe them on the front of the shirt. That's an absolute no-no. Wiping on the tablecloth is an even worse sin. Which cuts down the options.

That's why someone invented the table napkin. Women love them. A woman can dine through a hurricane with a napkin serenely resting on her lap. But a man's napkin is on the floor before his hand reaches the fork.

Even if a man could keep one of the blasted things on his lap, the average napkin is about as effective in coping with sticky fingers as a blotter on the Exxon Valdes. So what's to be done?

The armpits? Forget it. Too visible. Pockets are better. For years I got away with that. I developed a technique. It wasn't civilized but it worked. When no one was looking I'd quickly dip my fingers into my coffee cup, discreetly drop my hand to my side and wipe my fingers on the inside of my pocket.

Ingenious—except it deteriorated pockets. Holes developed. That was my downfall. I asked Mrs. H once too often to sew up a pocket.

"How come," she demanded, "your pockets keep wearing out?"

"I don't know," I said. "Maybe they just don't make 'em like they used to."

That didn't satisfy her. She kept on boring until she wormed the truth out of me. And once she knew what an uncouth savage she had married she trumped the news to everyone within earshot.

"My husband," she said, "uses the inside of his pockets for a napkin."

I felt like two cents. Even worse I had to find another way to deal with the sticky finger problem. I switched to the top of my socks. It took a long time for her to catch me. When she did it was newscast time again. She was on the phone to our daughters for the better part of an hour that evening. "Guess what," she said. "The old goat's wiping his fingers on the top of his socks."

They all had a good laugh. I was out of options. Last Sunday we were eating breakfast. It was a Wheaties and toast breakfast—hardly worth carrying into the dining room for civilized dining so we perched on stools at the kitchen counter.

Wouldn't you know the toast leaked butter all over my fingers. It was a moment of truth. There were two choices. I could either get up and wash my fingers at the sink or find something on which to wipe them. I had to make a decision. I could feel her eyes upon me. She was watching my every move.

Now I am not devoid of culture. I can be genteel. I can be a man of manners when I set my mind to it. With exaggerated motions so she'd be sure to notice, I reached across the counter and plucked a paper napkin from the holder. Very slowly I wiped the stickiness off of my fingers.

"See," I said, "I didn't wipe my fingers on my shirt. I didn't tuck them under my arm. I didn't shove them in my pocket. I didn't swipe them around my socks. I got me a napkin from the holder. Aren't you proud of me?"

"Any reason why you didn't use the one I set there by your plate?" she asked. I looked down. It was right where she had left it.

"Oh," I said.

Lew Hudson

Our Columnist Might be a Quack

There's one big reason why I don't want to see the snows come. It's the same every year. As soon as it snows, people begin to kid me about the way I walk. Not people in general, just my family.

They say I walk like a duck. Mrs. H says, if there was snow on the ground, she could trail me all the way across Minneapolis.

The fact is, I point my toes out a little—but just for traction. Cross country skiers do the same thing going up steep hills. If they didn't they'd slide backward two ski lengths for every one they took forward.

"But you do it downhill," she says.

Which is true. It's the main reason I have trouble water skiing—one foot goes east and the other goes west and pretty soon I end up in the lake.

Actually, I've always been a little suspicious of people whose feet line up. Notice the trail they make in the snow. Parallel strips. It looks sneaky.

Then take a look at the trail I leave. Mine is more friendly. It meanders peacefully this way and that. The biggest problem is accidentally tripping people.

The other day we were being shown to our table in a restaurant.

I stepped to one side to let a busy waitress by. Unfortunately not all of me did. My left toe lagged. Sure enough, she stumbled over it and almost dropped her tray.

Penguins, I told Mrs. H, have been doing pretty well for eons and they walk funny like me. Ducks too, I said, and geese.

She wasn't too impressed. She started ticking off creatures that walk with their feet pointed straight ahead—horses, cows, deer, chickens, grasshoppers, cats, squirrels—just to mention a few.

She had the courtesy not to mention frogs.

"At least I'll never lose you," she said. "A blind bloodhound with a head cold could follow your trail."

Eating Dinner Can Be Such a Struggle Sometimes

There are three kinds of people in the world—those who like carrots, those who don't and those who think everyone should. For the record, Mrs. H is among the first group, I'm the second and the waitresses at the Holiday Inn are in the third.

We were having dinner there the other evening. Carrots were vegetable of the day. When my plate arrived, there was a big, ugly pile of them despoiling the view. Lori, our waitress, knows my aversion to orange food but she's heartless. "They're good for you," she said.

That's easy enough for her to say. She likes carrots. When I was a kid, every time I objected to carrots, Dad would solemnly pontificate, "Eat what's before you and say nothing about it."

Many's the time I've sat at the table long after everyone else was gone trying to muster sufficient courage to gag 'em down. Mom used to claim they were good for the eyes. "Did you ever see a nearsighted rabbit?" was her favorite line.

Personally I'd rather skip the carrots and wear glasses. This time, though I was stuck. Lori wouldn't take the orange blobs back to the kitchen in trade for something edible. I studiously avoided letting any juice from them contaminate the mashed potatoes when Kim, another waitress, breezed by saying those who don't clean their plate can't have dessert. "And that includes carrots," she advised.

That's another thing my mother used to say. Mrs. H meanwhile, was enjoying herself. "These are good carrots," she said. Good carrots is a contradiction in terms. It's like saying fresh lutefisk or a little bit pregnant. By this time, half the people in the restaurant knew there was a struggle going on and were watching to see whether I caved in.

You'd think that by the time a man gets to be 64 years of age he should be able to decide for himself whether or not to eat carrots. Disliking carrots, though is perceived in most circles as a threat to public health and vaguely un-American.

So what did I do? The same thing any red-blooded citizen of these United States does when 50 people are watching to see if he's going to live up to his responsibilities. I ate my carrots.

For a moment I thought I was going to get a round of applause. Mrs. H smiled. Lori was happy. Kim was proud of me. "Now you can have some dessert," she said.

"Thanks anyway," I said. "I'm so full of carrots, I don't have room."

Pig Headed Can Mean Big Trouble

Back during the political season I heard a candidate in one of his less thoughtful moments refer to his opponent as "pig-headed". That got me thinking of the time several years ago when Mrs. H and I spent a few days of vacation on the Iowa farm where she grew up.

The place had been in her family since the Civil War and in some respects it looks like it. The barn and sheds are old and the fencing questionable at best. In fact, my nephew describes the place as being open range, although not by design.

Mrs. H's brother lives there alone. On the day of our visit he was substituting for the rural mail carrier so the two of us were in charge. That, as things developed, was not an apt description of our status. We were having a leisurely breakfast when a commotion broke out in the yard. It didn't take long to analyze the problem. The pigs were out.

Now these were not a bunch of slow-moving, contented old sows. These were a dozen or so frisky, 159-pound porkers, and they were enjoying themselves immensely. Some were in the flower beds, others in the garden, still others in the yard and four or five running down the drive, grunting with delight.

We went out, hoping to arrange a meeting with the escapees

and engineer their surrender. That was a laugh. These pigs weren't much in the mood to talk, although Mrs. H was doing pretty well on her part.

About that time, one of the neighbors came over to help. Using a pickup truck we eventually got ahead of the far-ranging critters and turned them homeward. For the first time in a half hour or more of chaos, we began to think order could be restored. We should have known better.

We had not yet been taught what it means to be pig-headed. Things were going smoothly. We had the whole bunch moving quietly up the drive toward the pen. The gate was wide open. All we had to do was run them in and get back to our bacon and eggs. Nothing to this farming business—or so we brashly thought.

Had someone drawn a straight line from one gatepost to the other, it would have marked the spot where the lead hog stopped. No way would he, or any other pig in that herd, step across that line. Hogs came up to the line, stopped and spun around, preferring to face pressure from the neighbor, Mrs. H and me. We were discussing the issue vehemently and backing up our arguments with clubs.

Things intensified as we advanced on the milling hogs, crowding them closer and closer against that invisible barrier. Not until we were able to force one of the animals across the line did the stalemate break. Once it did the others quietly strolled in, turning to eat as if nothing had happened.

Pig-headed? It is an epithet not to be bandied about lightly. It is one that should properly be reserved for real insults. Pig-headed is not just stubborn. It is more than that. It is irascible. It is totally uncooperative. It is independence to the point of irrationality—reveling in it.

Oh, For the Good Ol' Days (OFTGOD)

Somewhere we took a wrong turn. In the old days inventor gave simple names to the products they dreamed up—telephone, train, radio. I shudder to think what they'd be called if they were invented today. Given our bent for obfuscation, the name of the telephone probably would be voice-actuated electronic wire-conveyed audio transmission device or VAEWCATD for short.

A train could well be an integral powered interconnected rail guided mobile processionary system or IPIRGMPS. Radio would be an electromagnetic audio synthesizing instant retrieval system or EASIRS.

I got to thinking about it the other day after reading an article in Smithsonian Magazine on how designers have screwed up our lives. The writer contended engineering has taken precedence over common sense.

He said designers with no concern for customers give us such things as remote controls that roll off tables, kitchen ranges that don't clearly show which switch operates what burner and car dashboard devices whose functions we can't begin to interpret.

The writer didn't get into the matter of instruction sheets

although he well could have. Most are apparently written by functionally illiterate foreigners and translated into English by inept dropouts from unaccredited correspondence schools.

We live in the age of the scientist. No one gives two whoops about customers. That's why we have such things as electronic devices whose controls we can't decipher and whose instructions for operation we can't understand.

That's why we are confronted with advertisements for 20 MHz 386SX 85 mb hard-drive personal computers with 2499-bps modems and VGA monitors although few of us have the foggiest notion what all that means. We've allowed modern life to be cluttered with devices we don't really want, scarcely understand and can't describe without the use of acronyms.

Small wonder our stress level is so high. I'm for progress and machines that make work productive and life easier. I'm against inept design, foggy instructions and unnecessary acronyms. I'm for simplicity. I'm for printers instead of dot matrix printing devices, screens instead of video display terminals and recorders instead of videocassette imaging machines. I'm for straight-forward English. I'm for calling a spade a spade rather than a foot actuated manually controlled leveraged solid waste elevator.

Or FAMSLSWE for short.

The Good Old Days?

The "good old days?" We're living in them. Consider what it was like a hundred years ago. During this month of July, 1884, the city of Minneapolis had 102 deaths from cholera, 22 from diarrhea and six from dysentery.

Four years earlier a report written about the city of New York spoke of "appalling" numbers of deaths of children in the lower tenement districts from diarrhea and malnutrition particularly during the summer months.

Until about 40 years ago, about the only treatment for pneumonia and tuberculosis was bed rest and prayer. Polio wasn't conquered until about 20 years ago and there was no real remedy for kidney failure until transplant surgery was perfected a decade or so back. Even cancer is giving grudging ground to scientific research.

These are the "good old days" indeed.

Lew Hudson

Don't Mess Around with Breakfast of Champions

I couldn't believe my eyes. There it was in black and white—an advertisement from General Mills that it is introducing a honey-glazed version of Wheaties. Honey-glazed Wheaties? Say it isn't so!

Why would General Mills want to do a dumb thing like that? Why fix something that isn't broken? Have Wheaties eaters been complaining? Have there been letters to the editor demanding honey-glazing? Have irate customers been storming stockholder meetings of Minnesota's corporate cereal giant? Have pickets been parading outside the gates? Has Ralph Nader been issuing critical press statements?

Of course not. The Wheaties recipe, developed by accident when someone accidentally slopped some cooked wheat bran onto a kitchen range, was perfect from the beginning. My grandpa ate Wheaties. So did my father. Wheaties were my first solid food. To this very day I faithfully greet the dawn with a heaping bowl. Occasionally I close the day the same way.

In more than 60 years I've eaten about three trainloads and never once have felt the need for honey glazing or the addition of raisins, nuts, twigs, pine needles or any other foreign substance.

Jack Armstrong wouldn't have stood still for this. Old Jack relied on the Breakfast of Champions to sustain him when the going got rough. He would have gagged on honey-glazed Wheaties.

And what about the athletes who have smiled from Wheaties boxes down through the years. Can you picture Michael Jordan eating honey-glazed Wheaties? You've got to be kidding. What about Bruce Jenner or Mary Lou Reton or Bob Richards? Would the Minnesota twins have won two World Series on honey-glazed Wheaties?

Honey-glazed Wheaties—the new Breakfast of Champions. Forget it. You might as well feed Ovaltine to the Chicago Bears. The pathway of history is littered with the wreckage of companies that toppled while reaching too far for the golden ring. Tail fins on cars, Nehru jackets, the Edsel, junk bonds—all are examples of what happens when well enough is not left alone.

If I had any General Mills stock I'd sell it quick. A company whose management would honey-glaze the most successful cereal in history isn't long for this world.

What next? Marshmallow Wheaties? For shame! Return to your senses General Mills. Admit your mistake. Recall every box. Burn 'em along with those responsible.

Buy some ads in the newspaper and apologize to your legion of faithful customers. Otherwise I'm switching to Kellogg's.

Man on the Street

Got to thinking the other day that it has been years since I've heard a man-on-the-street radio show. Most radio stations used to have them. They'd send some guy downtown every hour to stop people on the street and get them to discuss various issues, or just to pass the time of day.

Henry Morgan, the comedian, had such a program when he worked for a station in Duluth. Duluth winters being what they are, it was tough on cold days to get anyone to stop let alone stand around and visit. Henry, they say, used to change his voice and interview himself.

I know how he felt. Years ago when I worked for a radio station at Oskaloosa, Iowa, I had three years of man-on-the-street duty. I can remember the days of near panic as the clock counted down to broadcast time with no one in sight. In case you've never tried to fill 15 minutes, it is a very long time to talk solo.

One hot August day it was broadcast time and there wasn't a single soul on the broiling sidewalk besides me. Luckily, five minutes into the show, an elderly gentleman came along. My only hope. No way was he going to get away. I stepped in front, grabbed his arm and brought him to a halt. He didn't really comprehend what was going on but after a while I got him talking. Then to my chagrin, he started pouring out a tale of physical woe the likes of which aren't normally discussed in public and I couldn't get him stopped. Things like that perhaps explain why we don't hear man-on-the-street shows anymore.

Words are Fascinating

Words are fascinating. Lugubrious literally sounds mournful. To say the word "bang" is to imitate an explosion. Sooth would be a calming word even it if mean something else. Dollup is a fair approximation of what it sounds like when you pour sorghum out of a jug. It's not hard to figure out how those words came into the language.

What's even more fascinating is the similarity between certain languages. Take the English word "three". It's tres in Spanish, trois in French, tre in Italian, Swedish and Danish, trei in Romanian, treis in Greek, trys in Lituanian, tri in Welsh, Russian and Yulgoslavian, drei in German and Dutch.

Linguists say all these languages are Indo-European, and stem from a single village or group of villages in Europe about 6,000 B.C., a Garden of Eden perhaps? People took the language with them as they migrated and changes evolved over the years much like English English and American English have evolved to the point where they are quite different tongues with basic similarities.

Lew Hudson

Strange Things Happen in the Night

How would you feel if you woke up to find that your right arm had grown two inches overnight? That's how I felt the other morning when I was putting on my bathrobe. I grabbed at the end of my pajama sleeve to keep it from scooching up to my elbow and couldn't reach it. It was two inches up my wrist.

Don't ask why I didn't turn on the light to see what the problem was. Rational thought isn't one of my strong suits at that hour of the day. I just jammed my arm into the bathrobe, scrooched the sleeve up to my elbow and stumbled out to the kitchen to tell Mrs. H she now had a husband whose right arm was two inches longer than his left.

It was fortunate her back was turned. I had time to examine the situation in the light before making a fool of myself. My arm hadn't grown. It was just that my pajama sleeve was turned back a couple of inches.

But discovering the reason doesn't explain how it happened. Someone—or something—rolled that sleeve up and it wasn't me. Strange things have a way of happening in the predawn hours around our house.

Take my eye glasses, for example. Every night when I take them off I carefully place them on a night stand. During the night they invariably burrow under the stuff I emptied from my pockets the night before.

I wouldn't mind if it was just my fountain pen or wallet, but when one bow is threaded through the key ring and the other intimately involved with the watchband, sorting things out can be a problem.

In the closet my house slippers also delight in playing games. I keep them in a special place—side by side in one corner of the closet where I can easily jam my feet in without turning on the light.

The other day I came out to the kitchen walking more like a duck than usual. My slippers were on the wrong feet. Now how could that be? They were lined up perfectly when I took them off. The older I get the more I believe in the witching hour. When we were kids we used to scoff at stories of toys coming to life at midnight. Now I'm not so sure.

Finding the truth though isn't easy. Scientists aren't any help. They don't work nights. Writers do but ask them about late-night mysteries and they say such things as, "Yes Virginia, there is a Santa Claus."

Police and sheriff's officers are up late, but they're always on the other side of town. I suppose I could ask my brother, David the Iowan, to look it up. He's a research librarian. But he still hasn't figured how library books trade places all by themselves. And there's nonsense in trying to keep watch. At my age I'm ready for beddy bye before the 10 p.m. news.

Which gives inanimate objects plenty of time to work their mischief.

Flexible Flyer

If there's a better sledding hill in all of Southwest Minnesota and Northern Iowa than the one behind the Christian School at Chandler, I've got to see it. Going by there the other day I stopped to watch a bunch of kids scooting down the slope, and they were yelling, screaming and having a ball. Some were on sleds, others on plastic toboggans and one or more on hunks of cardboard. It was all I could do to restrain myself from getting the snow shovel out of the car trunk and going up there myself to give it a try.

It sparked memories of the favorite sledding hill of my boyhood days. It was at a placed called "Toad Hollow", about a block from our house. In those days plastic toboggans hadn't yet been invented and wooden ones were far too costly for common folks. Since we were about as common as they come, for us it was either scoop shovels or lids.

For a long time the only sled we had was an ancient family hand-me-down "Eskimo". Then came the Christmas when we got a "Flexible Flyer." When I say "we" I mean "we" because I had to share it with my older brothers. That sled, though, was the king of the hill. It set records that were the envy of the neighborhood for maneuverability, speed and distance.

It's mine now and hangs in the garage, unused since my own kids grew up. When I got home from Chandler the other day I took it down and admired it. It's still a beautiful sled. Wonder if the kids at the school would mind if I tried it out just once on their hill?

Compass Points Right Way

When Alexander Pope wrote, "As the twig is bent, the tree is inclined," he must have had parents in mind. When our son, Frederick, was about five we were vacationing in Canada camping on Caliper Lake not far from Nester Falls. One afternoon we decided to drive into town to shop.

It was an old family custom. Whenever we vacationed we made it a point to let each child pick a memento even though it wasn't always easy to keep their wants within the limits of our finances.

Those were the years when Fred would have given anything to have been old enough to go deer hunting. Every fall he saw me off with sadness and greeted me home with joy.

One of the things I never failed to have with me when deer hunting was an old brass compass that had belonged to about three generations of my family.

On this particular shopping trip Fred decided it was time he had a compass, too. The trading post had two different kinds. One was a simple brass compass for about $3. The other was a mapping compass with a sighting device for about $4.95. He liked the elaborate one. Our budget favored the simpler one.

The clerk put both out on the counter for comparison. Fred and

I discussed their merits. I was leaning strong for the brass. Little by little he came my way. Finally he agreed.

The clerk wrapped it up. I paid the $3. Before we were out of the parking lot Fred had it unwrapped. "Dad," he said. "The man gave us the wrong one."

Sure enough he had. The clerk had charged me for the brass compass but had inadvertently wrapped the more expensive one.

"Come on Fred," I said, "we'll have to take it back." He was disappointed but obedient. We made the exchange.

I promptly forgot about it. Fred didn't.

Years later we got a letter from one of his teachers. In it was an essay Fred had written as a class assignment. "I just thought you'd like to see it," the teacher said.

Tears filled our eyes as we read. It was about the compass incident. Fred wrote that it had taught him a lesson about honesty; that no matter what the circumstances, it is dishonest to take advantages of someone else.

"I didn't understand at the time," he wrote. "Now I do."

"Tis education forms the common mind. As the twig is bent, the tree is inclined."

It's a Father's Day lesson for all of us.

Dispatches From Our Corner of the Globe

Long Trip Spurs Random Thoughts

    Random thoughts following a long automobile trip: 80,000-pound semis are pressing out deep parallel grooves in the right-hand lanes of Interstates. Even on dry paving they cause cars to swerve this way and that. When filled with water they're dangerous. Can't wait to see what happens when they're icy...

    I like the entry sign at Lockhart, Texas, saying, "If you lived here you'd be home now". Out in Texas range country they post signs saying "Loose Livestock." Our farmers sometimes have that problem too, but they don't generally advertise it.

    State tourism people should get together with their highway departments and make sure at least the first mile of all entry roads is in good repair. Nothing gives a worse impression than to come off a smooth road onto a washboard at the state line.

    Vigorous enforcement has finally slowed freeway traffic in Oklahoma and Texas down to 58.

    Texans display their state flag everywhere. Minnesotans don't.

Lew Hudson

Christmas Comes Early This Year for Mr. H

I think I've got it figured out. You've heard me mention it before —Mrs. H's fabulous record of winning drawings. Mine is the opposite. Other than her I haven't won anything in years. Until last week. One of the local stores held a pre-Christmas showing of ornaments. It's our custom to buy a special one each year so we went over to have a look. While there we were invited to register for ornaments they were giving away as door prizes.

Usually I let her sign us both up. I tell folks the only reason I married her was my need for a secretary. That's always good for a laugh. This time, though, I picked up one of the blanks and filled it out myself. I don't know why. It just came over me.

Last week they called to tell Mrs. H she had won. That was no surprise. She usually does. But when she went over to pick up her ornament there were two of them—one in her name and one in mine. Imagine that! A prize for me! A special award!

I couldn't believe it. Out of all those slips they drew my name. Why me after all those years? It's a mystery. At least it was. I got to thinking. It dawned on me that a person's chances go up proportionately with the number of slips in the box. A person who has her name in the box twice doubles her chance. The fellow whose name isn't in the box is zilched.

Could it be? All those years when she filled out two slips—could she have been putting her name on both? I asked her. She just smiled. "Isn't it a nice ornament?" she said.

The Power of Negative Thinking

It isn't easy being a Jonah. People tend to look askance or walk across the street to avoid meeting face to face. I know about these things. My power of negativism is immense.

The other day I tuned into the Gopher-Purdue football game just after the Gophers had taken the lead in the fourth quarter. Four plays later Purdue was back out front and the contest was over. Blame me. I'm used to it.

All season it has rained regularly in Baxter. The week after Labor Day I seeded the scars left by the sewer excavators in our yard and other than a few sprinkles it hasn't rained since.

I wash my car, it rains. I pick an election favorite, he loses. I'm responsible for the Twins collapse. One evening back in late July I had nothing better to do and watched part of a game. That was that for the 1992 season.

I planted sweet corn in my garden the year the western corn rootworm first appeared in Minnesota so there is every reason to blame that on me too.

Last weekend my brothers were in town. I took them out for our annual fall fishing derby and in so doing ruined angling in the entire northern half of Crow Wing and the eastern half of Cass

County.

The secret of success is to keep me out of the game.

Three or four years ago I was in Iowa City the Saturday afternoon that the Gophers were battling Iowa. As usual, our side didn't have a chance. My brothers, Hawkeye Bob and David the Iowan were pouring it on unmercifully.

I knew the only way I could help the Gopher cause was to refrain from either hearing or viewing any part of the game. When my brothers went to the TV, Mrs. H and I went shopping.

In Iowa City it isn't easy to avoid a Hawkeye football game. Every bar, every store, every house, every office, every pedestrian and every kid in a stroller has a radio blaring.

As we walked by a downtown bar an animal roar inside bulged the windows. We assumed the Hawkeyes had scored although we didn't dare ask.

At the mall, every store had a radio on. Several times I had to put my hands over my ears to ward off the jinx. We couldn't even go into Penney's because it was on the store's loudspeaker system.

To make a long story short, I safely avoided hearing a single word and the Gophers won. I'm sure glad I have Mrs. H. Her positive vibes dampen my negative ones. Otherwise, we'd never catch any fish.

Dispatches From Our Corner of the Globe

Secrets of the Trade

Picked up the Sioux City Journal Monday and read where Cy Douglass was dead at the age of 86. Cy spent a lifetime at news reporting, most with the Associated Press. His bylines included the Valentine's Day gangland massacre in Chicago in 1929 and the visit to Iowa of Soviet Premier Nikkita Khrushchev in 1959, but that's not why I remember him. I remember him because in one afternoon, Cy taught me more about being a reporter than I ever learned in journalism school.

He was AP bureau chief in Des Moines and I was a young reporter at one of his member radio stations. There was a terrible school bus crash in which 10 children died. I called Cy when the story broke, promising him details as they became available.

Thirty minutes later I was getting nowhere because every law officer was at the scene and unavailable. About that time the AP teletype at my elbow began chattering and here came Cy's story—names, ages and parents of the victims—eye witness details—the name of the teacher—the school they attended—the works.

When I called him back to ask how he did it he just laughed. "The old corner drugstore trick," he said. He explained when he worked Chicago in the gangland days there'd be a shooting about every night. As soon as they'd hear about it on the police radio they'd look up in the phone book the neighborhood drugstore closest to the scene and give them a call. Invariably there'd be someone there who had gone past the scene and stopped in just bustling to talk about it. They'd get the story even before the police picked up the body.

On the accident story Cy called the closest rural telephone operator and asked her to ring someone living out in that neighborhood. He got a woman who lived across the road and who knew everyone and everything involved. I can't count the number of times I've done the same thing since and for that matter, taught other young reporters the technique. Cy would have liked that.

A Rose by Any Other Name

It's been an epidemic in recent years of this sort of thing. Janitors have become building maintenance advisors, colleges have become universities, secretaries are word processing specialists and the old unemployment offices, after going through a series of name changes, have evolved into the Department of Economic Security.

The job accomplished is, of course, more important than the title. For example, I can still recall the name of the janitor in my grade school down in Iowa. He was Mr. Sullivan. Everyone—kid, teacher, parent or administrator—knew that Mr. Sullivan was a man without an enemy, a man who was proud to be a janitor and a man who was so good at it he needed no other title to add prestige.

Mr. Sullivan's name I remember, but try as I might, I can't recall the name of the guy who had the title "principal" lettered on his office door.

Chapter 4

A Sporting Chance

Dad harbors a great love and respect for nature and the out of doors. He instilled in each of us that notion of reverence for the world around us: lakes or forests or rolling fields. An avid bird watcher, Dad also has been a hunter of duck, pheasant and deer. He taught us to leave nothing but a footprint on the paths we trod. He possesses a keen competitive spirit as well and taught us everything he knew about basketball and football and other favorite games. The rivalry between his Minnesota Gophers and his brothers' Iowa Hawkeyes is ongoing and has yielded some interesting antics on both parts. It goes without saying that nearest to Dad's heart is fishing and there is no way to calculate the endless hours that he spent sharing that passion with his family.

Lew Hudson

Fishing Wasn't a Spectator Sport for Grandpa

Somewhere along the line fishing became a spectator sport. It didn't used to be. People used to go fishing because it was fun. If anglers watched each other it was only to see what the other person was using for bait or how deep the fish were running.

Fishing, not spectating, was the goal. That was then. This is now.

Today, fishing is big business. Tournament fishing draws crowds and sponsors. It's also entertainment. TV fishing shows compete for ratings.

Under the eyes of television cameras, factor-supported professional anglers hurtle $30,000 boats over waves at break-neck speed to reach favored spots ahead of the competition. Once there, contestants reel fish to the boat as fast as possible to minimize non-productive time.

Big bucks tournaments abound. Angling superstars smile for the cameras, wave to adoring crowds and negotiate lucrative endorsements.

There must be a couple dozen syndicated professional angling shows on TV, including of course, Brainerd's own Al and Ron Lindner and Babe Winkelman.

There's nothing inherently wrong with this, or course, but fishing was never intended to be a spectator sport. Like sex, fishing was designed for doing, not watching.

The problem with making it a spectator sport is that it makes the catching more important than the fishing.

My Grandpa—the greatest angler I ever knew—didn't see it that way. He treasured every minute on the water. Thinking about fishing was a pleasure. Talking about it was a delight. Going fishing was reward enough. Catching was just a bonus.

With all due respect to Al and Ron Lindner, Babe Winkelman, Gary Roach and the other TV anglers, their shows are entertainment, not sport. Through editing they compress three or four days of fishing into a 30-minute flurry of unceasing action.

That's a far cry from how life on the lakes is really lived. There are days when fish don't bite. Just once, for the sake of honesty, wouldn't it be nice if the pros admitted getting skunked?

Lighten up a little, guys. Laugh more. Swap some jokes. Tell a story. Find something more imaginative to say than, "That's a good 'un." Give us some variety in the way fish are photographed. Let us hear the views of a female angler once in a while. Take a kid with you. Better yet, take two and get some practice untangling lines. And start wearing life jackets.

You're role models now. Besides, you can always use them for commercial endorsements.

Baseball: an All-American Sport?

So now it's baseball season. Between now and sometime in late September each major league team will play 162 games to decide which of them will have the right to compete in a series of games to decide which two will compete to determine which is the country's best.

They'll call it the World Series but, of course, it won't be. Teams from the rest of the world aren't allowed. Not that they'd want to. The world's favorite game is soccer, a contest noted for action.

Baseball, on the other hand, is a game noted for inaction—about three hours of it interspersed with 12 to 14 seconds of action. In between about all that happens is that batters menacingly wave their clubs, fine tune their stance and look intently toward the pitcher.

Pitchers hitch up their pants, adjust their caps, dust their fingers with rosin, roll the ball around in their hands, stare intently toward the catcher for advice and glance over the shoulders to see if, by chance, anyone else is doing anything.

Usually no one is—except for spitting. Baseball players are the spittingest people in sports. No other athletic activity presents such a disgusting spectacle. Everybody, with the possible exception of the batboy and the play by play announcer, has a bulge in the cheek.

Managers and players sit in the dugout and spit. Pitchers dampen everything but the ball and sometimes that too. Batters stain home plate. Shortstops darken their gloves. Baseline coaches lubricate everything within 10 feet.

No one is concerned over elapsed time. I once knew a play-by-play announcer who claimed he left his broadcast booth, strolled down to the restroom and returned without his listeners even being aware he was gone. What's more they didn't miss anything.

Only in baseball could it take four out-of-zone pitches to issue an intentional walk. Why not just wave the batter to first base? On second thought, that would eliminate some of the game's more suspenseful moments. After all, there's always the chance a batter might decide to run over and swing at one of the throws.

Only in baseball is breaking the rules by doctoring the ball with nicks, scrapes or scratches looked on as honorable.

Only in baseball can a team be 34 games out of first place and still get a write-up in the newspaper as if it had engaged in a legitimate sporting event.

Only in baseball are the statistics more exciting than the game itself. Baseball has the greatest lobby in the world. I never knew a sports writer who wasn't devoted to the game.

To hear them tell it, baseball is the all-American sport—right up there with motherhood, apple pie, the flag and robins.

If that's true, did you ever stop to think what that says about America? Other sports have adjusted to the age of television. Baseball lives in the 19th century.

Auto racers go 500 miles in the time it takes to play nine innings. Football teams allow only 30 seconds between plays. Basketball has a shot clock. Curling has its energetic sweepers. Hockey and soccer players at least work up a sweat.

Baseball could be improved too.

Let batters decide for themselves whether to swing. Eliminate warm-up pitches. Install a 20-second pitching clock behind the catcher. Count it a ball every time the pitcher throws over to first base to check a runner. Count foul balls as strikes. Put a 10-second

time limit on infield conferences.
    And put spittoons in the dugouts.

Lew Hudson

Nightcrawler Picking Takes Talent

If you don't know anything about nightcrawlers you wouldn't understand the three-line want ad that showed up last week in one of the area papers. It said, "Wanted, reliable nightcrawler pickers," and gave a telephone number to call. Picking nightcrawlers might seem to some like an unusual occupation but not to people who run fish bait shops. To them a stable supply of the oversized angle worms is vital and there is only one way to get them in the numbers desired.

That is to go out at night and pick them. About an hour after dark the worms crawl out onto the surface of the ground seeking others of the species who might be romantically inclined. Conservative creatures that they are, however, they keep their tails firmly anchored in the ground in order to make a quick get-away if necessary.

That's what fooled my grandfather back about 1938 or so when he came to visit. He didn't know anything about nighcrawlers. They didn't have any in his town but he quickly recognized their superiority over common angleworms.

We kids took him out to hunt nightcrawlers one night. Taking care not to shine the flashlight directly on them because light can spook them, we pointed one out to Grandpa. He casually reached down to pick it up only to have it snap back into its hole so quickly it seemed to just disappear.

"I thought sure there was one there," he said. We let him do it a couple more times before letting him in on the secret. Successful nightcrawler hunters plop their hands down quickly on the worms to hold them in place and then carefully put stead pressure on them to make 'em let go.

Leeches Can Be Beautiful

To most people, passage of the Labor Day holiday means farewell to summer and hello to fall. To those who fish, however, it has a deeper significance.

Cooler weather means minnows can be kept alive in floating buckets and leeches can be moved from the refrigerator to the back porch. That's a relief for some people. It's surprising how many have an aversion to leeches in the refrigerator. Admittedly, they look a little out of place but that doesn't justify some of the reactions we've seen around our house.

House guests have blanched upon seeing a container of leeches next to the cold meat. Once Mrs. H would have joined them in a dash for the bathroom but, thanks to a lengthy educational process, she has been enlightened.

In the beginning neither of us was a leech person. We used minnows exclusively, but minnows can be a pain. They die for no apparent reason, and they aren't strong enough, big enough or nasty enough to discourage nibbling perch.

Leeches are, but the first time I suggested we try them, she flatly refused to even consider the idea. "Yuck" was one of the nicer things she said. I persisted until she agreed to allow a container of leeches in the boat, providing I kept them out of her sight. I did, but there was no way I could hide success. When I began to catch more walleyes than she did, she was quick to notice. She's not used to that.

The day I caught a four-pound walleye and she didn't, she reconsidered.

"Would you put one on my line?" she asked. I was happy to oblige. It was one of the few times in our married life I really felt needed.

A few trips later, she discovered that leeches attach themselves to the plastic lid of the container and, if care is taken, they can be hooked without being touched.

Still later, I came out of Lucy Nesheim's place one day with some particularly juicy leeches. Mrs. H said, "Those look like nice leeches." Catching herself, she added, "I can't believe I actually said that."

I don't remember exactly when she took the last step toward confirmed leechdom, but it was sometime during the next fishing season, I looked up from baiting my own line to see her gingerly reach into the container, pick out a big black one, hook it deftly, pry its mouth off her thumb and drop her line overboard.

I was so happy I leaned over and gave her a quick kiss.

After that, leeches became her favorite bait—and not without good reason. Now I have to fight her for the big ones. My brother David, the Iowan, has not yet achieved a working relationship with leeches. He barely tolerates night crawlers.

His wife, Kay is in the same boat and when they came up for a few days of fishing, we tried to introduce them to leeches. It didn't take. Volunteering, Mrs. H said, "I'll hook 'em for you."

That day's leeches were a lively and hungry bunch. They squirmed, coiled and attached themselves to everything within reach. I noticed David looking a little seasick although the water wasn't rough.

I've always felt a little protective about David. I've looked out for him since he was a kid. So I wanted to be helpful—to settle his queasiness if I could. "Just think of them as live liver," I said. Mrs. H laughed. David didn't.

Fishing Outfit Belongs to Mrs. H (Period)

Let's just say I didn't really know her. The spring after we were married I decided to buy Mrs. H a nice fishing rod and reel for her birthday. Not that we had anywhere decent to fish. Our first outing was to the Skunk River, an aptly named drainage ditch in southeastern Iowa. Our best catch was a 12-inch sucker.

We had only one outfit between us—the old Great Lakes steel rod and Shakespeare True Blue reel I had inherited from my father. The reason I inherited it was that he didn't want it any more. The handles had fallen off.

I made a couple of new ones from a wood dowel. They looked a little rough but worked. We took turns. She'd answer one bite and I'd take the next.

It was on the way home that I made the decision. If we were going to be spending the rest of our lives together it was obvious we'd be investing a fair amount of that time fishing.

A man and a woman, I reasoned, shouldn't have to share fishing tackle. A marriage is based on equality—joint tenancy bank accounts—share and share alike—equal fishing tackle. That sort of thing.

Besides, it would make her happy. That was the only thing in my mind. So off to the store I went. I picked out a springy steel rod about five feet long. It had a nice whip to it. Not too springy, not too stiff. Just right. It fit my hand like it was custom made. I selected a nice Shakespeare reel. They matched perfectly. "Sold," I said.

This was the outfit for her. It cost a bundle, but nothing was too good for my wife. Of course it did make my outfit look tacky. My homemade dowel handles were rough but they were serviceable. And my old rod did have a permanent bend.

But I didn't mind. I could struggle along until such time as we could afford something better. It was the least I could do. She was happy when she opened her gift. "It's beautiful," she said. "Just what I always wanted."

And then I added hopefully, "Sometime when you feel more like cooking or sewing or cleaning house than going fishing maybe I could borrow it."

"Sure," she said with a smile. "Sure."

Forty-one years have come and gone. We have become the Romeo and Juliet of fishing. No man has ever had such a devoted fishing partner. She's on about her fourth fishing outfit.

Her old rod and reel is in the garage. It hasn't been used for years. And never by me.

Bert Had a Way of Getting Even

Bert was an old friend, one of those persons who never took himself—or anyone else, for that matter—too seriously. He took equal enjoyment in laughing at and being laughed at. In the 20 years I knew him, we did a lot of laughing—both ways.

The only thing predictable about him was that you could count on him to be unpredictable. One cold November evening while Mrs. H and I were having supper, the doorbell rang. It was Bert. "Come on out to the car," he said. "I've got something for you."

Out at the curb he fished a key from his pocket and unlocked the trunk. There, all laid out in a row, was a limit of the nicest late-season bluebills you'd ever want to see. All were plump from gorging on wild rice from the prairie lakes of Manitoba and Saskatchewan.

He picked up a couple by the necks, hefted them and said, "They're for you. Considering how you shoot, I know you seldom get any ducks."

I thanked him, assured him they would be on our table for Thanksgiving and went back into the house to finish eating. When the dishes were done, Mrs. H and I went down to the basement to pluck 'em.

Ever since we've been married, I've made a point of assuring Mrs. H she's the world's second-best duck picker. It makes her feel good to be rated so high and encourages her to work even harder to improve her ranking.

Feathers were flying and the exposed duck lice were scampering for cover when I began to notice something about the duck I was picking.

"Where," I asked Mrs. H, "is that duck of yours shot?"

"The pellets are all in its back," she said.

"That's strange," I said. "Mine's the same way."

Next day I looked up old Bert. "Bert," I said, "not that I didn't appreciate the ducks, but I'm an old duck hunter and there are only two ways a fellow can shoot ducks in the back—either they were flying upside down when they went over or you sneaked up over the bank and dry-gulched 'em on the water. Which was it?"

His face reddened. "Well," he said, "I did sneak up and let 'em have it on the water."

We had a good laugh but, as it turned out, not the last. Bert saw to that. It took a while but he got even.

The next spring there was an uncommonly hot day in June. The temperature was in the mid-90's with the humidity about the same. There wasn't a breath of air stirring except in a huge, black thunderstorm building in the western sky and it hadn't come within reach yet. I came home from work tired, hot and decidedly disagreeable.

There on my front porch was a plastic pail half full of dead and dying crappies.

"Bert stopped by and left you some fish," Mrs. H explained. "Isn't that nice?"

I am known around our house as the world's second-best fish cleaner, an honor for which Mrs. H doesn't even compete.

Considering the heat and the rapid deterioration of the crappies, there was no time for dillying or dallying. I got out my filleting knife and went to work with the direct assistance of every fly in the neighborhood. A great guy, Bert. You should have heard him laugh the next day when I looked him up to let him know how much I appreciated his thoughtfulness.

"That's OK," he said. "Considering the way you fish, I know you seldom get any."

His words had a familiar ring. He didn't have to spell it out. The score was even—Lew 1, Bert 1.

Lew Hudson

A Picture-Perfect Angling Adventure

 The name is Mudd. Mrs. H and I were vacationing with friends last week at Rainy Lake. Fishing was great. Even the catching wasn't too bad. Walleyes were slow but bass were hitting off the rocky points and northerns cruising the weed beds.
 The northerns were running between three and four pounds with a few a tad larger. Bass were averaging three-quarters to a pound and one-quarter. Our biggest was about 2.5 pounds.
 The northerns were so hungry a couple even offered me a second chance. One missed on an initial swipe but connected when I cast back to his swirl. Another swirled about 50 feet from the boat but took the lure when I cast it his way.
 The bass were equally cooperative. Once as we cruised slowly past a rocky point, I let my ego get the better of my judgment and confidently boasted I would take a bass when my lure reached that point.
 They all laughed—until the bass hit. It was that kind of a week, but I'm getting away from my story. Mrs. H was trolling her favorite Shad Rap. In her view, there's only one lure that rivals Shad Rap, and that's another Shad Rap.
 Anyway, a northern inhaled it and the fight was on. It was the

best fish of the week. While she wrestled with it I grabbed for my camera. A couple of times she got it up to the boat only to have it dive under.

As soon as I got the camera set and focused, I said to her, "Take him around again so I can get a better picture."

"OK," she said.

"Bring him to the surface where he'll show," I said. "That's the way Al Lindner does it."

"OK," she said.

She worked him back to the surface where he treated us to a splendid head shake that rattled the hooks.

That's when I snapped the picture. Just as I did so, he dived under the boat. A second or two later her Shad Rap floated to the surface. Things got pretty quiet in the boat---but it didn't stay that way very long.

Mudd's the name. Photography's my former game.

One Man's Philosophy on Hunting

Ours has been a hunting family. Both Mrs. H and I come from long lines of outdoors people. Our three daughters and one son grew up with the sport.

Some of them enjoy it and some do not but all understand that, if there is to be meat on the table for Sunday dinner something has to die on Saturday.

It is never a pretty process. When you come right down to it, though, there is very little difference between the death of a chicken or steer and that of a grouse or deer except that one takes place in a slaughterhouse and the other in a forest.

I have never forgotten the first creature I killed. It was a cottontail rabbit. My conscience hurt. It still does every time I pull the trigger and bring a bird or animal to Earth. But remorse is only one of the emotions of hunting. It needs to be balanced against others.

Hunting involves instincts and feelings that are as old as mankind—the satisfaction of providing sustenance for loved ones, the companionship of the chase, testing of ones abilities, appreciation for nature and affection for all wild creatures.

There is a growing chorus of people who take the position

hunting is no longer necessary. They are probably right, if welfare of wild creatures is the only consideration.

Human beings however, are part of nature, too, and many of us need to play out the traditional role of the hunter. We are not yet a fully civilized species.

In the era of Bambi, when all wild creatures are perceived as possessing human characteristics, it is difficult to maintain reality. How, for example, could one shoot an animal that talks? How could one eat a bird that has a wife and children at home?

The world is not like that. Animals, while undeniably beautiful, don't talk or have human personalities. Birds don't marry and send their fledglings to college. Nor do they all live harmoniously in idyllic surroundings. The natural world is a harsh one in which the big exploit the small, predators kill and eat, climatic extremes extract a severe toll, starvation is a frequent reality and death of one sort or another is the eventual fate of every creature.

The farther people get from farms, lakes and forests, the less likely they are to remember and pass these truths along to the children. Present criticism of hunting is but a minor portent of what will come.

It is not impossible that hunting opponents will predominate and the sport will be legislated out of existence.

Wise hunters, by their sportsmanlike conduct, will avoid giving anyone additional reasons for taking such a step.

Application of the traditional rules of sportsmanship distinguishes true hunting from mere killing. The killing is the result of the hunting, not the reason for it.

If you haven't explained that to your sons and daughters, perhaps this column will be helpful. It's something we should all bear in mind as we plan for the opening of the deer season.

CHAPTER 5

Holiday Follies

Holidays of any sort have always been special in the Hudson family. Birthdays, Valentine's Day, Fourth of July and Halloween are held with great esteem and celebrated to the fullest extent. But held most dear in all our hearts is the Christmas season. Tradition held that Dad would first read the story of Christ's birth from the Gospel according to Luke every Christmas Eve. Listening to those words echo in Dad's deep voice made the miracle of Christmas come alive for us all. That was always followed by his unique rendition of Clement C. Moore's, "The Night Before Christmas." I am confident that Moore would have not been offended in the least by Dad's embellishments to that cherished poem.

Lew Hudson

Dispatches From Our Corner of the Globe

Tree Offers Plenty of Meaning

We have two family trees at our house. One is in a book on genealogy written by my brother, Hawkeye Dave. The other is in a stand next to our fireplace. Of the two, the green one is more fun. At the top is the 50-cent plastic angel we bought the first year we were married. Now, years later, she's something of a fallen angel. Every year we see new ones—some far nicer and all infinitely more expensive—but we wouldn't dare replace her. We'd have a revolution on our hands,

Near the top is an old bulb, the lone survivor of a string that was on my first Christmas tree. Nearby is a candleholder from Mrs. H's first tree in the days before electricity on her family's Iowa farm.

There are three Christmas card cutouts. One shows a brunette, one a blonde and the third a girl with sandy hair—each resembling one of our daughters. We chose each the year they were born. There's a shiny white ornament, especially chosen and hand-lettered in red the year Fred joined us.

Mrs. H and I have added a few others almost every year. Each has its own story to contribute to our tree's history. The two fragile hand blown ornaments were given to us by two elderly Swedish ladies who not only put up with the noise of our three rambunctious children when we lived in an apartment above them but who also adopted the girls as honorary nieces.

There are two etched glass discs—limited edition ornaments from Texas that remind us of happy times with the friends who picked them out for us. We bought the straw ornament at a little Swedish town in Kansas. The handmade ceramic ornaments remind us of happy days with folks who made them and who were like an aunt and uncle to our children.

At the end of one bough is the lavishly decorated ornament we spotted one time on a close-out table two weeks after Christmas and picked up for a song and about 20 cents cold cash. Here and there on the tree are Mrs. H's Santa Clauses. Each recalls the antique shop or gift occasion that produced it.

There's an antique wood child's block of the type that was commonplace 100 years ago. We bought the set at an auction when the kids were small. Scattered over the tree are the half-dozen candleholders a friend brought from Germany the year we had a candle lit tree.

Especially for the grandchildren are three of those enchanting mobile ornaments that have become so familiar. And a new addition this year is a spectacular hand-blown crystal ornament we picked up on the spur of the moment because it was so breathtaking.

All are illuminated by the strings of miniature red lights that have been our choice for as long as either of us can remember. I am a sucker for Christmas but I try not to let on. My annual reading of "A Night Before Christmas" is filled with outrageous modifications designed to mask my true feelings. It never works. The kids see right through me.

I guess it's the ornaments that give me away. I sit by the hour, gazing at them. The longer I look, the schmaltzier I get. Our family tree isn't a sterile, black and white record of ancestors living and dead. It's a sparkling, living record of our family's yuletide history, and its glow out the window is our merry Christmas wish to each and every one of you.

Some Guys Can't Be Wise Men

Directors of Sunday school Christmas pageants have some of the same problems as NFL coaches—what do you do when people get too old to perform? It's not easy. When are boys too old for a role in the pageant and what do you do when they reach that age? It's a tough call.

Make a mistake of forcing retirement too early and you have to deal with proud parents. Wait too long and everyone in church knows you goofed. The safest thing to do is designate them wise men. Wise men have nothing to do but dress up in fancy robes and parade down the center aisle bearing gifts of gold, frankincense and myrrh.

That's simple enough. Fairly safe, too. Even an eighth-grader can't do much other than stumble a time or two to foul up a kingly procession. At least that's what the pageant director thought several years ago in the church Mrs. H and I attended in Worthington. Boy, was she wrong. Every Christmas, people still recall how wrong she was. It's etched forever in the holiday lore of that congregation.

While Scripture doesn't say how many wise men there were on that first Christmas, the familiar hymn places it at three. Since the trinity has a good theological basis, people have generally accepted three as the traditional number.

On the evening in question, the pageant's wise men were three junior high boys—one named Paul and the other two named John. All three were in the twilight of their Sunday school pageant careers.

Their parents and others referred to them more often as wise guys than wise men but, because there was no other role in the pageant for junior high boys, they were elevated to kingly status and given marching orders.

They were to walk sedately down the center aisle, carrying gifts and singing the hymn, "We Three Kings of Orient Are." The procession had to be very slow in order to give each boy time to sing a verse describing the gift he bore. Between verses, they were to join in the chorus.

The pageant was going fairly well. There had been only one minor incident between a couple shepherds to mar tranquility at the stable. Out in the foyer, the wise men lined up. Beards and mustaches were on reasonably straight, dim light obscured the frayed hems of their robes and their gift packages were presentable.

At the appointed time they started out. The first verse—"We three kings of orient are," was magnificent. After that it was downhill all the way. Starting the second verse, one of the Johns forgot the words. He also lost the pitch. Search as he might he could find neither.

That, of course, destroyed the thinking processes of his companions. They might as well have been singing, "Home on the Range."

Paul's verse was up next. The best he could do was, "Dum de dum de dum dum de dum." When verse three came, the other John couldn't even remember "dum de dum." All he could do was babble incoherently.

Initially, people snickered nervously. As the musical carnage continued however, snickers changed to muffled laughs and when those could no longer be contained, to uproarious guffaws. Gales of laughter swept the church.

It no longer mattered that the three were making up words as they went along. No one could hear them anyway. They got back together—almost—for the final chorus while parishioners reached for handkerchiefs to wipe tears from their eyes.

It was truly a night to remember—graduation exercises for John, Paul and John –the last Sunday School Christmas pageant of their lives.

Memories of that program came flooding back a week or so ago. Mrs. H and I were shopping at Brainerd mall. There, in one of the stores, we ran into one of the members of that wise-guy trio. We hadn't seen him for years. We greeted each other and surrounded by Christmas decorations, it was only natural this famous old tale came up for the retelling. We shared a good laugh.

I told him I was going to write a column about it. He shuddered. I said I'd be nice and not tell anybody his name. He said he'd appreciate that. He was a man who has a reputation to uphold. I'm a man of my word. There are a lot of people named John living around this area and you will note that's the only name by which I have identified him throughout this column. Incidentally, if you're not familiar with the old hymn, "We Three Kings of Orient Are," you might ask the band director at Pequot Lakes High School how it goes. I'm sure he remembers it now.

Lew Hudson

Halloween Tricks Are a Treat to Recall

Next to Christmas, Halloween was the favorite holiday for kids of my generation. For a few glorious evening hours, all restraints on juvenile conduct were removed. We reveled in it. We roamed our town like a pack of mongrel dogs. No window was safe from soap, no outhouse sacrosanct, no home off-limits.

Ours was not a trick-or-treat town. It wasn't until I was a grown man that I heard of little urchins actually giving grownups a choice in the matter. We were tricksters, pure and simple.

Small wonder then that our children grew up loving Halloween. We enjoyed it together. To hear them tell it, their father was the strangest character in the neighborhood on Halloween. They might have been right. My spirits still stir when the sun goes down Oct. 31.

Halloween stories abound in our family from those years. Like the time we sneaked over to our neighbor's house, tied a black fishing line to his storm door knob, looped it around a couple of trees and took the end to a hiding place. Then we rang the doorbell. When Dr. Moore ("Chuckie" as he was known to the kids, even when they were in his English classes in college) came to the door, it opened mysteriously, untouched by human hands. I'd have given $10 for a picture of the look on his face.

Another year we took a bucket of black dirt and, by judiciously spreading it, created an instant grave, complete with headstone, in his front yard. By some strange quirk, the photographer at the newspaper heard about it and the whole town enjoyed it on the front page the next day.

Our oldest daughter and I dressed up one night in masks and capes, hid behind an evergreen tree and waited for some innocent trick-or-treaters to ring our bell. When three little ones came along we silently and suddenly loomed up behind them in the darkness. There wasn't a dry pair of pants in the trio.

Another Halloween, carrying water buckets filled with shredded paper, the whole family raided the home of some close friends. That one backfired. While Mrs. H and I in costume stood expectantly at the door ready to heave a couple buckets of "water" as the door was opened, our friend Merle, who had spotted us out of the window, ducked out the back door, sneaked around the side of the house and grabbed one of our daughters, lurking there in the darkness. It took a week for her nerves to settle down.

I can't remember whether it was our son Fred's junior or senior year in high school, but his gang concocted the idea of swiping and stockpiling plastic bags of leaves awaiting refuse pickup. Halloween night they hauled hundreds of them to the high school and filled a courtyard about six feet deep with leaves. School authorities, momentarily nonplussed, made a lot of dire threats. Parents just chuckled.

Actually, Halloween is one of our oldest holidays. According to Prof. John Sherman of Moorhead State University, it goes back 2,000 years to the Celtic festival called Samhain. Celts believed that on that night, the dead literally came back to mingle with the living. While people might have welcomed ancestors and departed friends, others of the dead probably were considered a bit creepy, which probably accounts for much of the scary stuff associated with the night.

A Smothered Christmas

Have we finally managed to smother Christmas? Some would say so. All would agree we've tried. The hucksters have given it their best shot. We've bought and baked until we're broke and bloated. We've wrapped and written until we're weak and wordless. And the holiday doesn't come until tomorrow.

But we haven't smothered Christmas. All we have done is cover it with tawdry trappings. The miracle that is Christmas is still there to be rediscovered. Some may find it in the smile of a child. Others may read it in the face of an old man or woman remembering the ghosts of Christmas past.

Sometimes a special ornament or reenactment of a family tradition may kindle it. At other times it is a Christmas card or a Bach chorale. Or the sound of an organ, violin, guitar or Salvation Army bell. It might be released when we break the seal on a Christmas card from a close friend or smell the fragrance of fresh-cut evergreen.

We may discover it in the crunch of newly fallen snow on a nighttime walk or in glimpsing a red wreath in a dark window. The spirit of Christmas appears in its own good time. We may not even find it at church on Christmas Eve. It may elude us, only to be revealed in the touch of a loved one's hand or in a quiet rereading of the Christmas chapter in the Gospel according to Luke.

But sooner or later it will happen. You can count on it. Sometime between now and the dawn of Christmas Day, a smothering layer of trivial trash with which we have covered Christmas will be rolled away. The miracle of Christmas will once again work its magic. Our world will once again be transformed into a very special place—at least for a few fleeting hours. Christmas is like that. It has always been.

The first Christmas was smothered too—almost lost beneath the trampling feet of thousands of people en route to their ancestral homes to be counted and taxed.

It was far from a perfect time for history's greatest events. No one—least of all those travelers—expected anything from that stable at the back of an inn. But something happened there, and the stable couldn't hold it. The miracle of Christmas burst forth and lighted the skies for shepherds, wise men and all of humanity to hear and see.

It was confirmation that almighty God, creator of the universe, reaches out in love to unlovely human beings. That is the miracle that is recreated every year at this time, and human beings play only a minor role in it.

Christmas is not a human event. Christmas is a spiritual event for humans. Humans can no more suffocate it than they can prevent the sun from shining. So relax. Christmas isn't humbug. And Christmas isn't smothered. It's well, it's Christmas—and that's all it ever needs to be. Rejoice. God loves you. Merry Christmas

She Wanted To Be a Christmas Star

How could you console a child whose primary ambition in life was to be chosen for the part of the Virgin Mary in the annual Christmas pageant?

We had such a child. She's in her 30s now. Many of her life's goals have been attained but she still hurts at Christmas when she remembers being passed over for the part.

First she was too young. They made her a member of the angel chorus instead. When she got older there were other excuses. She was blonde. The Virgin Mary needed dark hair. She sang too well. The choir couldn't spare her.

There were other girls who were better actresses. Of course they never came right out and said so, but she knew. Every year it was a new excuse.

Any bumbling clod could be Joseph. Joseph didn't do anything but stand there gazing into the manger. Any awkward kid could be a shepherd. Shepherds didn't do anything but lean on their crooks.

Angels were a dime a dozen. White gowns and golden halos transformed even the homeliest.

Wise man—even those who couldn't remember the second verse of "We Three Kings"—were forgiven of their trespasses.

But everything revolved around the Virgin Mary. She was the focal point. All eyes were on her while the narrator intoned the familiar words from Luke.

And our daughter wanted that role. It was her childhood ambition and she longed for it. Her sisters would have been flattered if asked but to them it was no big deal. But this one wanted it. She coveted it.

"Why can't a blonde be the Virgin Mary?" she asked. "She wears a shawl over her head anyway."

There was nothing Mrs. H or I could do. We weren't the directors. We had nothing to do with the casting.

Time after time we talked about it. Maybe next year would be different. Maybe one of the glamour gals would come down with the chicken pox or get a hickey on her nose and open the way for our daughter to become a Christmas star.

Only it never did. She was in the pageant every year. She sewed costumes. She helped with the staging. She sang. She played her violin. She narrated. She cleaned up when it was over.

Every year she looked forward with anticipation and backward with dejection. Every year she was just one of the people in the crowd, but she loved Christmas.

She always has. She still does. Every year she bubbles with December excitement. She bakes and sews and sings and buys and wraps and gives.

She is Tiny Tim, Bob Cratchett, Rudolph, Santa Claus, the Christmas angel and the ghost of Christmas present all wrapped into one.

But never the Virgin Mary.

Chapter 6

Politics as Usual

Dad's career as a journalist led him down many different avenues. He reported on murder trials, automobile crashes, train derailments, fires and endless civic issues. Though generally a mild-mannered man, his demeanor could change much like Clark Kent's when he was faced with an issue about which he strongly felt. For example, in the 1970s he campaigned tirelessly for the Highway 60 four-lane project which today, some 40 years later, has nearly reached its completion. Other issues he merely pondered and pontificated about in his weekly columns.

Lew Hudson

Things Aren't Like They Used To Be

What's going on?   In this country we used to arrest those who sell pornography.   Now we can't even keep it off prime time television.

We used to say the country owed a debt of gratitude to war veterans. Now we bill them for hospital care.

We used to value freedom as sacred. Now we equate it with license.

We used to celebrate our cities as melting pots of civilization. Now, they've become cesspools of hate.

We used to institutionalize the mentally ill and retarded. Now we turn them out and wonder why there are so many street people.

We used to think it only fair to help single mothers raise their children. Now we demand they get a job and wonder why their children didn't turn out better.

We used to build jails to hold criminals. Now we turn them loose because jails cost too much.

We used to proudly support national charities. Now half-million dollar executives squander our donations.

We used to seek political leaders with a vision for the future. Now we choose them on the basis of 20-second sound bites on the evening news.

We used to place service before self. Now we settle for the opposite.

We used to consider schools investments in the future. Now we view them as expansive drags on our present day lifestyle.

We used to rise up in righteous indignation when a political leader violated our trust. Now, we're so angry over other things we just let it pass.

We used to think we had the capacity to correct any wrong. Now we lack the courage to even try.

We used to believe in a day's pay for a day's work. Now hiring part-timers to avoid paying fringe benefits is commonplace.

We used to idolize athletes who played for the love of the game. Now we lavish affection on those with the largest paychecks.

We used to accept responsibility for our own mistakes. Now we retain an attorney and go to court.

We used to encourage career employees. Now we terminate them at their peak because they make too much.

Sacrifice and compassion are becoming alien concepts. Indifference and apathy are proliferating. Accountability and responsibility are diminishing.

What's going on?

TV News Reporting Has Changed

Remember when TV news people used to sit there with their eyes askew reading from TelePrompTers? They'd never quite look directly at the camera and it gave the viewer a peculiar feeling. It's better since inventors came up with those transparent TelePrompTer screens. On the other hand, it's getting worse for the weather reporters.

All that electronic gimmickry they use now to flash temperatures, cloud symbols, cold and warm fronts, thunder and lightning, jet stream routes and severe storm areas onto the screen requires weather reporters to watch themselves on a monitoring screen.

It's not like the old days when Ken Hirsch could stand in front of a panel with his telescoping pointer and tell us what was coming. Now, since the symbols are flashed onto the screen electronically, they stand there gazing toward an off-camera monitor, awkwardly trying to make their hands point to the right spots. It sure looks silly.

Russ Van Dyke down at Des Moines used to give about the best weather report in the business and the only tools he had were a keen mind, a marking pen and a transparent screen through which he could look directly at the viewer.

Are We All Capable of Murder?

Last time I counted I have come to know 23 murderers in my reporting career and by and large you couldn't ask for a nicer bunch of people.

There was one exception—a distant relative who chose an axe to do her dirty work. She wasn't nice at all. Other than her though, and she was a mental case, I've found murderers pretty decent people.

That's probably because the murderers I've dealt with were people who committed their crimes in fits of anger or while under the influence of drugs or alcohol. I've never known any sadistic killers of Mafia types who did it for profit.

The murderers I have known were pretty ordinary before and after they committed their crimes. In between, circumstances overpowered them and they surrendered to irrational conduct. With the exception of my distant relative, all were remorseful for what they did.

Although no one condones murder, least of all me, it can happen when human beings are pushed too far. While the limit varies with the individual, I have a nagging suspicion that the capacity for killing lies deep within each of us.

I remember one fellow who killed his wife and his mother-in-law, whom he contended broke up his marriage and prevented him from seeing his children. He looked forward to his trial as a chance to tell his side of the story.

Just before sentencing, the judge granted his request to speak. After an emotional 20-minute outpouring from the witness stand, he stoically accepted his sentence, went to Stillwater Prison and served his time. The last I heard he was out and living a normal life. Circumstances that made him a killer are extremely unlikely to occur again. Statistically, murderers are not recidivists.

Although most offenders are eventually freed, only the community can accept an offender back into society. Sometimes that is difficult.

In the course of my work I have seen the insides of many jails and prisons. I have looked through inspection windows into solitary-confinement cells and observed human beings caged like animals.

I have talked with inmates in their cells and tried to sense what it might be like to spend weeks and months behind bars.

I have drunk coffee with inmates and listened to their stories. Few with whom I have talked have held any delusions about their own guilt. All were human beings with friends, family, wants, needs, goals, ideas and feelings. Many were remarkable, intelligent —some truly perceptive.

As a reporter I have also stood with notebook in hand and watched what has happened in dozens of police stations and sheriff's offices. I have seen far more than I have reported.

Years ago, in a city many miles from here, I watched two police officers subdue a disorderly drunk by using his head as a battering ram against a desk. The blood poured as they dragged him to a cell.

I have seen defendants brought into court with telltale bruises on their faces and have listened to officer's joke about how people sometimes bruise themselves falling from jail bunks.

As I look back I have to share some of the blame for such excesses because, in the interest of preserving news sources, I did not expose what I witnessed. Like the officers involved, I rationalized my conduct.

Fortunately most law officers maintain higher standards now. It is well they do. If there is one thing I have learned from these experiences it is that all human beings can err—even those who carry badges.

It isn't often that I get serious in this column but sometimes all of us need to be reminded how easy it is to call for vengeance and how difficult to extend understanding.

After showing me through a prison once a warden said, "We don't have any bad people here—only people who have done bad things." I never forgot that.

Lew Hudson

Who Can Forget?

Remember Pearl Harbor? Those who were alive that day do. They remember the terse radio bulletin. They remember shocked telephone calls from friends. They remember the outrage.

A half century later they still remember the 2,300 Americans who died. They remember the crippling blow to the Pacific fleet. They remember the four years of brutal warfare that followed. They remember the 407,000 dead and 670,000 wounded Americans.

The people who lived that war remember how the United States transformed itself into the world's foremost military power.

They remember the 16 million veterans who, when it was over, transformed this nation into the world's foremost economic and political power.

They remember rebuilding the ruins of Europe through the Marshall Plan, restoring a shattered Japan through the patient leadership of General Douglas MacArthur and formation of a United Nations to prevent it all from happening again.

That World War II generation was remarkable, perhaps unique. It was a generation whose collective civic and moral values were spawned in the modern world's worst depression and forged in history's biggest war.

Molded as it was by such momentous events, its members see things through different eyes than those who grew up in the societal quicksand of the 1960s, '70s and '80s.

Those who were privileged to have seen a truly unified nation are uneasy with purposeless fragmentation.

Those who offered their lives don't understand those who offer their country nothing.

Those who challenged and defeated German Nazism, Italian fascism and Oriental fanaticism have little tolerance for dictatorial despots.

Those who carried the stars and stripes to the farthest corners of the world have no time for those who defile it to make a political statement.

Those who remember Pearl Harbor, Bataan, concentration camps, refugees and carpet bombing can be excused if they don't feel guilty over use of atomic bombs to decisively end it.

The World War II generation cries for humanity but remembers clearly who started it.

Remember Pearl Harbor?

Who can forget a day that lives in infamy? Who can forget the anger? Who can forget the sight of determined men lined up at recruiting offices? Who can forget rationing, war bonds, scrap drives and casualties? Who can forget told star flags and flag-draped coffins?

Who can forget nightly reports of daily battles? Who can forget tragic headlines? Who can forget battlefront maps? Who can forget the concentration camp walking dead? Who can forget the sight of emaciated prisoners of war?

While this nation has made some mistakes in its history, World War II was not one of them.

The young men and women who forcibly exorcised a genuine evil from the world are not silver-haired seniors.

Hatred has faded. Memories have not. Remember Pearl Harbor? Heaven help us if we ever forget.

A Start on 'Hudson's Book of Proverbs'

Last October when I turned 60, I officially became a senior citizen. Yes, I know, the American Association of Retired Persons accepts 55-years into membership but that's jumping the gun. No 55-year old with an AARP card is going to impress a restaurant cashier in charge of ringing up senior citizen discounts.

I've been waiting for this a long time. Now that I am a senior citizen, I can start advising people. I tried giving advice when I was about 30, and you should have heard them laugh. What could a young squirt like that know about anything, they said.

They were probably right. Now, however, it's different. They may still laugh but no one can call me a young squirt. Age doesn't confer wisdom of course, but most seniors have accumulated enough bruises and abrasions to know a little about how the universe works.

In anticipation of this period of my life, I've been working up a list of pithy sayings to compile someday into a book. I think I'll call it, "Hudson's Book of Proverbs". That has a nice ring and I don't think King Solomon's copyright is still valid.

From reading his Book of Proverbs, I got the impression that he didn't start writing until he was about my age. Because that was about 2,500 years ago, some of his observations are a little dated.

Not all, of course. Some still have a ring of truth like this one: "Tis better to live in a corner of the housetop than in a house shared by a contentious woman."

Not having done that I can't speak to the accuracy of his observation but I imagine it is as valid now as it was in the old days. Solomon, however, couldn't have foreseen all of the vexations afflicting human beings in later years. That's where "Hudson's Book of Proverbs" comes in. It's sort of a sequel. I don't think Solomon will mind.

Hudson's proverb No. 1 reads: "Thou shalt discover, my son, that machine designers who create troublesome work areas are infinitely more skilled than are those who attempt to overcome them."

Had Solomon lived in the modern world and barked his knuckles a few times trying to loosen a hidden bolt, the wisdom of that saying would certainly have struck him.

And, had he been a retreater rather than a conqueror, he would also have learned as I have that wise men never burn their bridges unless they happen to be retreating—or advancing to the rear, as it is sometimes described.

Here are some others I'm contemplating:

"As quickly as you learn the rules, they will be changed."

"Whether you are hanged with a new or an old rope makes little difference."

"You will learn, my son, that whatever products you particularly like will be taken out of production forthwith."

"Waste not thy days worrying about the national debt lest thou become the only one so engaged. Instead spend thy days worrying about thy personal obligations over which though hast some measure of control."

"Whatever tastes good, if not already banned, will eventually be declared bad for your health."

"Whenever thou casteth thy nets at one end of the lake, the fish will be clustered at the other. There is no way thou can outguess them, even with an electronic fish finder, an Al Lindner book or a Babe Winkelman video."

"When all else fails and Mille Lacs Lake walleyes have you buffaloed, seek out Joe Fellegy."

"When angling, whichever side of the boat though shalt cast thy line into will be the one with the snag."

"Though shalt learn to thy regret that the more thou needest money, the less anxious thy banker shall be to see you."

"And, when thy days grow short, though shalt realize that, to have loved and lost is about the same as to have lost a love."

Mrs. H thinks I should keep these things to myself—that I sound like a pompous old fool. Personally I don't feel the least bit pompous.

Lew Hudson

Budget Restraint Should Be Taught to Lawmakers

She's starting to see the light. When they were little our kids never really understood their father. They couldn't fathom why he dismissed every roadside attraction as a tourist trap and kept on driving.

A deer farm? Sorry, I didn't see it in time. Time to eat? I'll pick the restaurant. Mid-afternoon lunch? Eating between meals is bad for your health. A gift shop? They sell the same sorts of things cheaper at home and besides you've already got a Barbie doll.

They complained, argued, pouted, plotted and despaired. An amusement park? What looked to them like a fairyland of carnival rides, novelty items and sumptuous food was to him just another tourist trap.

What they didn't know was why. It never occurred to them that money spent on unexpected had to be made up elsewhere if we were to get back home to Minnesota.

If governments budgeted as tight as we did they'd send checks to taxpayers. When you walk into a restaurant with a $5 budget and $10 worth of appetites it takes powerful persuading to convince children they really don't need fries with their noon burgers to survive until supper time.

That's why on our trips we specialized in scenic vistas, waterfalls, locks and dams, rivers, lakes, hills, cliffs, forests, trails and relatives.

Relatives don't charge room rent. Our kids grew up knowing their cousins. At one time or another they slept with most of them. I still can't get over the habit. Mrs. H has been wanting to stop at a tourist trap down toward St. Cloud but the traffic is always too heavy or we're short of time or I'm past the turn-off or whatever else in the way of an excuse I can dream upon the spur of the moment.

Of late, though, I've begun to think our Pine River daughter, Cindy, is beginning to understand her father. She's even beginning to sound like him:

"A can of pop?"

"Later, maybe. Not now."

"A big California burger?"

"You can't eat that much. Why not just a plain one?"

"Stop at the Coyote Corral?"

"We don't have time."

"A motel?"

"Camping would be more fun."

Like father, like daughter, I always say.

Like Father Like Daughter

It's getting scary. Our daughter Rebecca has started a column in the Murray County News at Slayton under the heading, "Smelling the Roses". Her topics are local events, whimsical comments, community gossip, humorous stories, fond recollections and observations about community life—the same sorts of drivel she has been reading in her father's column for years.

The scary part is when she starts to reminisce. It's one thing for parents to write about their children, but quite another for a former child to write about her parents. Mrs. H and I await arrival of the newspaper with mixed emotions.

Once she wrote about the day she got her driver's license and asked her mother for permission to take the car over to her girlfriend's house. Mrs. H, not quite ready to surrender her daughter to a dangerous world, suggested that since it was such a windy day she'd be better off riding her bicycle.

I enjoyed that one.

Then she wrote about some of the strange things I do with food —like keeping peanut butter in the refrigerator, putting a little sugar on chocolate pudding for grit and mixing Cheerios with Wheaties to create Wheatoats.

Mrs. H thought that was hilarious.

Now we're both wondering what she will think of next. Will it be Mrs. H's collection of empty boxes, second hand ribbons and left-over Christmas paper or my collection of canceled checks, paid installment contracts and jugs of used motor oil?

A Little Plagiarism is Just Innocent Fun

First it was Senator Joe Biden whose presidential candidacy succumbed to hoof in mouth disease. Then it was U of M Acting President Richard Sauer who made the mistake of quoting a well-turned phrase without identifying its source.

It's getting so that you have to be very careful. Out in the woods, it seems, people are scrutinizing every public utterance and waiting to pounce like hungry tigers on hapless victims.

For the record, I didn't make that up. I heard it somewhere.

Fortunately we haven't always been so picky. When Albert Einstein first reported his theory of relativity, no one called him to task for failing to say that one of the basic formulas used in its calculation—two plus two equals four-- wasn't his.

Someone has said that Thomas Jefferson, when accused of having borrowed some of the loftier phrases he used in the Declaration of Independence, told his detractors to bug off—he was helping form a government, not teaching creative writing.

Do you really think Julius Caesar was the first person to write, "All of Gaul is divided into three parts"? Not likely. Chances are he lifted that from a report filed by one of his lieutenants who had just returned from a junket out that way.

John F. Kennedy surely wasn't the first person to declare himself a Berliner, yet he got away with doing so on the day he visited the Berlin Wall.

Many times, when covering court proceedings, I've heard people declare, "I am not a crook." Even so, I don't remember Richard Nixon being criticized for plagiarizing those words in his now famous explanation for Watergate. Maybe everyone was laughing so hard that they forgot to raise the issue.

People have been plagiarizing for years. Coin designers unabashedly copied "E Pluribus Unum", and "In God We Trust" so many ways that no one remembers or really cares who said them first.

Do you really think Irving Berlin dreamed up the words, "God Bless America?"

Has anyone credited the author of those memorable words, "Kilroy was here?"

Ned Buntline, I think it was, wrote, "Smile when you call me that, pardner," but did you ever see him get a screen credit when John Wayne or Jimmy Stewart used it in the movies?

I think I've heard at least eight scholarly sermons on love, and they all used Paul's words on the subject because no one has ever said it better.

By this time, most worthwhile things have been said. It's tough dreaming up fresh phrases. It's one thing to lift someone's manuscript and palm it off as your own. That's despicable. On the other hand it's tough to find fault with a little borrowing here and there.

A little knowledge is a dangerous thing, but a little plagiarism is just innocent fun.

I read that a long time ago—about four score and seven years, I recall.

There's a Right and a Wrong Way

Someone was holding a meeting the other day and since going to meetings is my hobby I was there. In fact I arrived a few minutes early.

I hung up my hat and took a seat in my accustomed spot—up front and to the right. Given a chance I always sit up front and to the right. It's something I've done as long as I can remember.

Mrs. H and I always occupy the same place in church—up front and to the right. When we go to a theater, concert, lecture, open forum or just plain old meeting—it's up front and to the right. Watching TV at home we're more comfortable if our chairs are toward the right and up close.

I can't remember a single time when we've gone anywhere and willingly sat toward the rear and to the left. Don't ask why. I don't know. It's just like that, of course. We have some friends who are both backward and left learning. We don't criticize. Who are we to judge? If they want to be different that's up to them. Naturally we always stop to say howdy as we walk by.

In a few minutes before the meeting started I found myself thinking about this phenomenon. What dictates where people sit at meetings? What obscure factors are at work steering people one way or the other?

Is it something akin to the force guiding migrating monarch butterflies or birds over thousands of miles? Is it psychological imprinting that occurs within a few hours of birth?

Could it be that our right or left delineation is determined for all time by whichever side the nurse places us when we are first presented to our mothers for nursing? Who can say?

Or does it have something to do with political persuasion? Are Republicans more inclined toward the right and Democrats to the left? That's logical, but it doesn't explain a preference for front or rear nor does it explain why some well-known Democrats were sitting on the right-hand side at this meeting.

No, there must be other forces at work here. Right- or left-handedness? Maybe.

Protective instinct that prompts chivalrous males to escort females on the side opposite their stronger arm? Perhaps.

Driving on the right-hand side of the road? Could be.

But if so that would mean the British would behave just the opposite. They may. But how could you tell? The British do everything just the opposite.

The herd instinct? Possibly. First person down may influence others. For whatever reason, more than three-fourths of the people attending that particular meeting came in the door, looked around, and took seats on the right-hand side of the room.

There was no discernible difference between those who strode in purposefully or wandered in aimlessly—between those who patted their hair into place as they entered or who stopped just inside the door to fish out their combs—between those who stopped to take off their wraps or who left them on—no difference. Most veered toward the right and sat down.

By the time proceedings started the room had a distinct list to starboard. Fortunately it was a boring meeting and I didn't have to take too many notes which left time to observe. I began to see things I had never noticed before.

As the meeting progressed it appeared the left-wingers were more restless and uncomfortable. They fidgeted, twisted their necks, coughed nervously, blew their noses, checked their watches, drummed their fingers and looked out the window. Some even got up and left before the meeting was over.

    Don't ask me to explain it. I don't even know why they were over there in the first place.

Lew Hudson

Chapter 7

Music Hath Charms...

The Hudson house has always been filled with music. As we were growing up, instruments of every kind abounded, and we all played one or more of them. Dad's music tastes run deep, from blue grass to polka, to big band and classical and beyond. He has even been known to tolerate "John Elton" as he dubbed this daughter's favorite performer. Dad's eclectic tastes in music led his offspring to the appreciation of many forms of music, both in the performing and enjoyment of it. This may perhaps harken back to the 50s when he was a disk jockey spinning records on the radio. Whatever the case, we always had a stack of 78- and 33- rpm records to enjoy on the hi-fi set in our home and knew every word to every song that the Chad Mitchell Trio ever recorded, and in recent years, both mom and dad have become integral members of their church choir.

Lew Hudson

Dispatches From Our Corner of the Globe

Harmonica Has Been a Good Friend

The harmonica has its artistic limitations but nothing equals it for happy music. I got to thinking about that the other day while talking to George Bedard. George and I are among the oldest harmonica players in the Brainerd Lakes region—maybe the world.

George didn't say how long he's been playing, but I've been at it more than 50 years.

I started shortly after striking out as a piano player because I wouldn't practice and as an oboist because I preferred football. One morning during my oboe days I showed up at band practice with my middle finger in a splint—broken the previous afternoon trying to make a tackle in a schoolyard football game. The band director said I'd have to choose between the oboe and football.

If he had it to do over again, he probably would have rephrased that. I continued football and switched to the harmonica. I played it through high school, in the Navy, occasionally during college and frequently when our kids were growing up. I still play it from time to time when the grandchildren are home.

I have a lifetime of harmonica memories. It helped the hours pass on lonesome nights during my Navy days. Later I cultivated the art of playing a rollicking tune while bouncing a kid on each knee.

Harmonica music helped the miles go by when we drove the Alaska Highway.

Notes from my harmonica echoed beautifully from the sheer walls of Santa Elena Canyon on the Mexican border in west Texas, when Mrs. H and I rafted the Rio Grande with two special friends and a guide who loved to sing.

It accompanied us on a midnight hay ride across a remote south Texas ranch. It inexplicably called walleyes to our boat on Lake Kabetogama one spring morning while my tuneless brothers a few feet away were skunked.

More than once it has played old favorites at family songfests. It has serenaded the setting sun at dozens of Minnesota and Canadian lakeshore campgrounds.

I'll be the first to admit there's no sound to equal a violin, no instrument more versatile than a piano and nothing closer to the soul than a guitar, but ounce for ounce and inch for inch nothing produces music like a harmonica.

What's more, once learned, the art of harmonica performance is never forgotten. My grandfather was a harmonica man. The first tune he learned was a jig called "Irish Washerwoman". He played it for me when I was a toddler and he played it for me when he was past 75 and short on breath.

The first number I learned was the old Jimmy Davis song "You Are My Sunshine." I still play it for our granddaughters. It's their favorite song and I'm their favorite musician—at least for now.

Bach, Handel, Mozart and Ravel are for orchestras. It takes a band to perform Sousa and King. For dancing, nothing has ever topped Glen Miller, Tommy Dorsey or Artie Shaw. It takes Jerry Lee Lewis or a Bruce Springsteen to hammer out rock 'n 'roll.

Acuff, Gilley and Travis are guitar men. Organs and choirs are find for Sundays. Just about every musical instrument except the harmonica has a special time and place.

No music has been written especially for harmonica. Jerry Murad and the Harmonicats are the only musicians I can recall who ever made a career playing it.

The harmonica is more at home in a barnyard than a concert hall—more comfortable in the hip pocket of a pair of old jeans than in a plush instrument case backstage.

Loved by no one except people, harmonicas persist generation after generation. Most musicians conclude their performing days upon graduation from high school. Not harmonica players. Their music stays with them until the day they die.

Lew Hudson

Classic or Popular? The Ear Knows

Now before I begin, let me say that no one enjoys classical music more than I do. I've enjoyed it ever since I took up the oboe in seventh grade. Through high school I spent many pleasant hours listening to the Sunday afternoon symphony broadcasts sponsored by Texaco.

I also enjoy popular and country music, not to mention the Big Band sounds of the '40s and '50s. What I object to is the elitism demonstrated by many classical music devotees, particularly programmers at public radio and TV stations.

There is opera and there is Grand Ole Opry, and seldom the twain doth meet. With the exception of Garrison Keillor and Austin City Limits, public radio and TV are classical music. Commercial radio and TV usually aren't.

The barriers are seldom breached—except during public stations' pledge weeks. During pledge weeks the talents of Willie, Waylon and Grandpa Jones are used to attract dollars. A clear case of crass commercialism. A lot of composers' and performers' talents are walled off from the people by classical elitism for which there is no historic precedent. Barriers between classical and popular would have been alien to many of the classical composers.

A Chopin polka played by the New York Philharmonic is the same dance as a Whoopie John Wilfahrt polka by the Six Fat Dutchmen. One is no more cosmopolitan than the other. The same for mazurkas, schottisches and waltzes by the Minneapolis Symphony and Chmielewski's Funtime Band.

Much of what is regarded as classical music today was popular music when it was written. Handel and Strauss wrote for the popular market and made a bushel of bucks in the process.

Many of Mozart's sparkling compositions were done to fill commercial contracts. Some of the best-loved portions of Tchaikovsky's Swan Lake ballet are the Russian, Siamese and Arabian folk dances. Folk dances are dances of the people.

The harpsichord featured so often on classical music programs was the favorite instrument of the people of its day. When the piano was invented people decided they liked it better and turned the harpsichord out to pasture.

Classical aficionados have been trying to put them back into harness ever since. One of the dreariest classical numbers in my collection is a harpsichordist presenting a couple dozen eight bar variations on an undistinguished theme.

Some of the classicists even borrowed from each other. There's a Beethoven piece based on variations of Handle's Conquering Hero theme from Judas Maccabees. After I listened to both I decided Handel had it right the first time.

How about a little more mutual respect in the music world? The various types aren't mutually exclusive. One is no more meritorious than another.

The key is what pleases the ear

Dispatches From Our Corner of the Globe

Tune In for the Latest Meadowlark Hit

From all indications, classical music is full of meadowlarks. After last week's column in which Mrs. H challenged my claim about hearing a piece of classical music whose theme was built around the song of the meadowlark, several readers rallied to my side.

Hank Hemquist of Baxter was the first to call. He said he's an old farm boy and the opening four notes of Beethoven's "Fifth Symphony" remind him of the song of a meadowlark. Well, maybe Hank, but I don't think I ever heard a meadowlark sing bass. Anyway, that was not the one I had in mind.

Nor was the one suggested by Jim Murrow of Baxter. Jim said Ferde Grofe's "Grand Canyon Suite" has a spot in which the song of the meadowlark is heard.

It comes, Jim said, in that portion of the suite where the orchestra vividly portrays a mountain thunderstorm. The kettle drums mimic thunder and the cymbals punctuate it with audible representations of lightning, while the violins and violas produce the sound of swirling winds. Suddenly, the storm abates and in the silence that follows, he said, off in the distance the violins and piccolos sound forth with the song of the meadowlark.

Jim said Mrs. M doesn't give him any credit for musical knowledge either. And, by the way he added, do you remember that other bird-song classic called, "Did You Ever Hear Pete Go Tweet, Tweet, Tweet?"

Yes Jim, unfortunately I do. Try as I might I've never been able to blot that one from my memory.

Robin Moede of Brainerd however, came up with what I think was the one I had in mind although I won't know for sure until I can find a recording and listen to it. She said she heard on a recent "Artists in Concert" program on KSJR Public Radio a Minnesota group called the Lark Quartet playing a composition by Minnesota composer Libby Larsen. The selection was titled "Alauda", (Latin for lark).

That number, Robin said, borrowed a theme from an older composition, Joseph Haydn's "Opus 64", which has as one of its central themes the song of the meadowlark.

Robin called Grand Music Co. of St. Paul to see if a recording of the Haydn opus is available. Unfortunately she was told, it is not in current issue.

The piece, I think, is the one I remembered. Mrs. H however remains unconvinced. "Not until I hear it with my own ears," she said.

Have You Heard 'Tingle, Tangle Brittle Car?'

There is a special glow in the faces of parents of string musicians. It comes from surviving years of torment.

The glow was there last Sunday when the Brainerd High School String Ensemble conducted by Grant Wilcox played Handel, Mozart and Beethoven for the congregation of First Presbyterian Church. Mrs. H and I shared a proxy pride in their accomplishment. Afterward we reminisced.

Our two oldest daughters were violinists. Our third was a flutist and our son a cellist and trombonist. All were orchestral musicians —first in grade school, later in high school and in the cases of the violinists still later in the community symphony. Believe me; nothing improves with age quite like a violinist.

And nothing has more room for improvement.

In the beginning every note is like fingernails scraping on a blackboard. Put two beginning violinists together and it sounds like a cat fight at midnight.

There is no escaping. The sound bores its way to the farthest corner of the house ripping and tearing eardrums as it goes.

In a desperate but futile attempt at muting, we fixed up a basement practice room. To lend it dignity we called it the conservatory.

"And please", we said," close the door". It helped only a little. In time we developed circles under our ears. We faithfully attended every public performance. Without parents, beginning musicians would play to empty theaters.

The first concert was ghastly. The class played "Twinkle, Twinkle, Little Star". It came out more like "Tingle, Tangle Brittle Car."

The second year was only slightly better. In the beginning, improvement for string players is agonizingly slow. As the poet has written, however, the night is always darkest before the dawn. By junior high, Mozart, Beethoven and Tchaikovsky began to assert themselves.

What has been an exercise in agony starts to become a blending of harmony. By high school, most string musicians have subdued, if not mastered, their instruments.

And that's when a special glow from the faces of proud parents begins to illuminate concert halls. Friends and neighbors begin to show up because they want to, not out of a sense of duty.

In a world where discord masquerades as music, there is something very special about a high school orchestra.

For the parents who have already been through hell, the concert was heavenly.

Dispatches From Our Corner of the Globe

Even Piccoloists Slam Oboists

Oboe players seem to be the Rodney Dangerfields of music—they just don't get much respect. Hardly had the ink dried Sunday on the column in which I admitted to having at one time been an oboist, when a letter arrived from my old friend, Hank the Ham of Omaha, calling the column a "literary effusion."

That surprised me a little. Hank doesn't usually use such big words.

Anyway, he said when he was considering studying music in high school, his teacher suggested anything but the oboe. The teacher said playing the oboe has a strange effect on the mind due to the effort it requires or something, and oboists get balmy in the crumpet. For that reason, Hank said, he chose the piccolo and played it three years. Three years? That's a long time to play an instrument for which there is a repertoire of only two selections. In our band the oboist—me—sat to the right of the piccoloist—Jack Leyde—and his playing made a lasting impression on my left ear.

To this day I can remember every note of the piccolo solo in "Stars and Stripes Forever," although I have trouble hearing them through my left ear.

The other piccolo song? "Yankee Doodle."

Lew Hudson

Memories of a Grave Digger

He's dead now so I guess it's okay if I talk about him. For that matter, he wouldn't have cared if I had talked about him when he was alive. What people thought or said of him was not one of his major concerns.

I went to his house one time to do a story on the trunks he built in his basement workshop. He made imitations of old, camel-backed trunks from scraps of wood and old aluminum printing plates he salvaged from the newspaper office.

He did a lively business—which was in sharp contrast to his regular line of work. By profession he was a gravedigger. Not the modern, scoop-it out-with-backhoe type of grave digger but an old-fashioned, pick-and-shovel excavator.

He brought to his job an uncommon devotion to excellence. As he put it, there is one time in a person's life when he shouldn't have to put up with shoddy workmanship.

He approached each job as carefully as an archaeologist. When he was finished the sidewalls were plumb, the corners square and the topsoil carefully placed to one side so it could be spread again when the burial was over.

He felt strongly that a fresh grave is scar enough in a cemetery.

A covering of black dirt allows nature to heal it more rapidly. He could go on by the hour spinning tales of bizarre cases of bones where they weren't supposed to be and fascinating incidents that had occurred in 50 years of funerals in which he played a crucial, albeit behind-the-scenes part.

Grave digging, although necessary isn't full-time work in a small town. A proper excavation, he said, was only a three-hour job in the summer. In winter when frost was three feet into the earth, it took a small charge of dynamite and six or eight hours with a pick and shovel to reach the customary six feet.

So he made imitation antique trunks as a sideline. He also was a shrewd antique dealer. Some folks used more descriptive adjectives. He lived near the edge of town where people were more tolerant of what he called his stock of merchandise and they called piles of junk.

We were walking out to a storage shed one afternoon to look at an antique bicycle when I noticed a dozen or more old-time cast iron toy cars and trucks scattered around in the snow. I said they looked too valuable to leave lying around outside. He smiled, stained the snow with tobacco juice and declared they weren't nearly as valuable now as they were going to be after they had aged a bit.

It wasn't that he was dishonest. It was all part of the game. He did business in Latin—Caveat emptor: Let the buyer beware. After all, most of his customers hoped to outsmart him and buy something at a fraction of its real value. He figured it was only fitting that he balance the books once in a while by unloading something at 10 times its cost.

He had a weakness for old fiddles. Over his workbench in the basement I spotted seven fiddle cases tucked away on an overhead beam. "Show them to me," I said.

One by one he took them down. There wasn't a whole fiddle in the bunch. Everyone was split and the discordant tones they emitted reflected that unfortunate fact. Even so, he was proud as punch of them.

Of course he wasn't so proud he wouldn't let one go for a price to some poor soul who didn't know that almost every violin has a slip of paper glued inside with written Italian saying something like Antonia Stradivari d'Cremons. If they couldn't read Italian and mistakenly jumped to the conclusion that "Stradivari" designated the maker rather than the pattern, then that was their problem.

"I'm not interested in a fiddle," I told him. "I'm an old banjo picker. Now, if you had a banjo, I might be willing to bargain a little."

"Well now," he said. "I think I just might." He went over to one corner of the basement and started digging through a pile of boxes and junk like a dog seeking a bone. Pretty soon he came up with a skeleton of an old banjo. It didn't have a head, strings or frets but everything else was there and all the metal fittings were brass. Beneath the grime the fretless fingerboard was decorated with hand-painted flowers in a style similar to Scandinavian rosemaling.

My mouth was a little dry as I casually looked it over. "It's pretty far gone," I said, "but how much would you want for it?"

"Oh," he replied, "have you got two dollars?" I couldn't believe my ears. Two dollars for this beautiful old relic? "Yeah," I said quickly before he could change his mind. "I guess it might be worth a couple of bucks."

Later, after I had polished up the brass, fitted new pegs and head and cleaned up the wood I got to thinking about it. Here was a banjo that was worth $200 or $300—maybe even more—and he let me have it for two dollars. It surely wasn't that he didn't know what it was worth. He always knew that.

Maybe it was just that he wanted someone to put it back in shape so it would once again turn out happy music. Either that or he had taken a liking to me.

I'll never know. He died before I saw him again. Reprobate that he was, the church was jammed for his funeral and the procession to the cemetery was more than a mile long. I never did learn who dug his grave.

Lew Hudson

Restlessness Shortens Opera Career

By the time a fellow gets to my age he can look back on a surprising number of mini careers. I was thinking about that the other day while having lunch with a couple old cronies.

I've already told you about my railroad career—eight long hours as a section hand on the Rock Island. But I've had lots of others—farmhand, greens keeper, advertising salesman, secretary, soda jerk, opera performer.

"Opera performer?" you say. That's what those two cronies said when I brought it up. "You in opera? Ha, ha ha!" That hurt. Yes I was an opera performer once. Not for very long, you understand, but an opera performer all the same. No one can take that away from me.

I was about 14 or 15. My brother Dick was four years older. Somehow he got the idea of hitchhiking 150 miles to Davenport Iowa, where our aunt lived, to see a performance of Verdi's opera "Aida." It sounded like fun. Our aunt agreed to take care of ticket arrangements and on the appointed day, we went.

Upon arrival we learned she not only had taken care of tickets but on the theory that we should experience what opera was like, had signed us up as extras.

Backstage that night one of the directors gave us instructions. A stage hand issued costumes and directed us toward a dressing room. When we came out, I looked at Dick and he looked at me. We agreed neither would strike fear into the heart of any sworn enemies of Egypt, but roughly speaking, we resembled what young citizens of Cairo might have looked like a few centuries back.

Before curtain time we listened as the performers warmed up and watched as they put on makeup. We got a chance to see how the sets were handled and looked over the lighting controls. But unfortunately, when the curtain went up for the audience, it came down for us.

Along with other extras who were scheduled to come on stage in the Grand March, we were herded into a back room and told to be quiet.

Before long my brother began to get a little restless. Here we had hitchhiked 150 miles to see an opera and all we were seeing was a backstage room filled with a bunch of bored people dressed in Egyptian costumes.

We not only couldn't see but we couldn't hear either. After about 15 minutes Dick blew up. "Let's quit," he said. "Let's change back into our street clothes, turn in our costumes and go out front to see the opera."

It sounded like a good idea, and that's exactly what we did. The Grand March that night was two people shy of a quorum.

We got to our seats in time to see about half the performance. Other than depriving the music world of our contribution to the crowd scene, nothing much was lost. I doubt if we were missed.

Now you would think that my two friends would have shown a little more respect after I told this story. Neither of them had ever been an opera performer. It was even questionable whether either had even seen an opera.

But they weren't respectful at all. They just sat there and laughed.

That hurt. I have never laughed at the outlandish yarns one of them habitually spins about walleyes he catches at Gun Lake. And I have
listened respectfully to the other's stories about flocks of pileated

woodpeckers attacking his bird feeder.

I was brought up to respect my elders and these two guys qualify. Their problem is they've lost faith in the integrity of their fellowmen.

Next time we have lunch I think I'll tell them about another of my careers-flying with the Blue Angels. They won't believe that either.

Some folks are just born skeptics.

Lew Hudson

Zippy Little Trombone Trio

Since Thursday's column about a Brainerd professional man who recently had trouble with the zipper on his trousers, I've come to the conclusion that similar stories probably lurk in mostly men's backgrounds.

At least that seems to be the case considering what some of my friends have been saying for the last couple of days.

In fact the unfortunate subject of Thursday's column volunteered a sequel that is even better than the original. I'm still not going to give his name. Wild horses couldn't drag it out of me. But he said that back when he was in school, he played trombone in the band. For the band's big indoor concert of the year he and two other fellows were scheduled to perform as a trombone trio. They practiced diligently and all was in readiness.

Unfortunately a trip to the men's room just before the opening number resulted in a jammed zipper and a problem worse than Richard Nixon's famed 18-mnute tape gap.

The three quickly forged a pact. The guy with the faulty trousers was supposed to stand in the center. He said flatly that wouldn't do it. It wasn't that he minded making a public appearance; it was just that he wasn't about to make that much of one.

Since there was no time to correct the gaping error, the other two said they wouldn't stand up either. There was, however, no time to tell the director.

The concert began and rolled inexorably along to the place in the program for the trio. At that point the director proudly turned to the audience, introduced the trio and announced their number. Nothing happened. They remained seated.

He announced them again, this time in a louder voice. Same result. A quick and heated conference followed at which direct threats were made—threats dire enough to prompt the trio to reconsider its position. Up they stood and to the front of the band they walked, the guy in the center lowered the music stand.

That just about broke up the party. The conductor started waving his baton, the band started playing and the trio chimed in. From that point on it was a mad race to the finish line to end the ordeal.

"We finished about three measures ahead of the band," my friend reported.

Chapter 8

Technicalities

From spinning 78 rpm records in the radio studio and operating a manual typewriter, to wrangling teletype machines and computers in the newsroom, Dad has deftly evolved with technology. He has never been intimidated by new innovations and has plodded boldly into the new age where technology rules. There have been moments, however, which shall remain as far less than stellar achievements for him. For example, disassembling and reassembling an ailing electric clock only to have it run backwards when plugged in was not exactly what he had planned. And adapting to the use of computer terminals in the newsroom was challenging, especially when "POOF!", the words he had labored over disappeared with the touch of a button into computer cyberspace. But by far Dad has adapted quite well considering the changes he has encountered along the way. Now if only he could program the VCR...

Lew Hudson

Zap! It's All in Knowing How, Dad

Somewhere along the line I lost control. I think it was about the time those video games came on the market. Before that I seem to recall our son Fred had some degree of respect for my abilities.

Not anymore. I think he still respects me but my abilities? No. At first I didn't do too bad. Donkey Kong was a reasonably simple video game and I could play it without too much embarrassment.

But then came other electronic contests. Zaxxon, for example. Instead of slow-moving barrels rolling down a ramp threatening to crush me as in Donkey Kong there were space ships on the screen—space ships that shot back. Using all the experience I had gained in 35 years as a private pilot I found I could dodge pretty good, but when it came to shooting the attackers my reaction time just wasn't up to it.

Fred's was. Not only that but he began to uncover secrets about the games no one explained to me. For example, he found safe levels for his space ship—places he could park, review the developing situation and then proceed to a strategic point from which he could score the big hit to send Zaxxon back to wherever it was he came from.

He even learned how to beat the system in Donkey Kong. He

claimed he didn't re-program the game but somehow or other when his little man got in a tight situation Fred did something with the controls that caused the barrels to start rolling off the ends of the ramps.

"How'd you do that," I asked.

"Nothing to it, Dad. It's all in knowing how."

It wasn't what he said so much as the way he said it—inferring that while old minds are all right for mowing grass and planting flowers only young minds are capable of absorbing video game technology.

I let it pass though on the disturbing possibility that he was right. But then came the day he borrowed the video game called Space Fury from a friend and brought it home. I have a sneaky suspicion he may have practiced a few times before he invited me to try out the new game. Either that or he's even sharper than I thought. Maybe both.

"It's a great game, Dad. You'll love it," he said.

Somehow or other I didn't really think I would but decided to humor him and give it a try. There's one thing Fred enjoys—being humored by the old man. He says he finds a lot of things to laugh about when he's around me.

Before we started he explained how the game works. The lever on the controller turns the little space ship around, the left-hand button is the thruster to move it and the right-hand button controls the zapper guns, he said. The idea is to turn the space ship toward approaching attackers and zap 'em to kingdom come.

That seemed simple enough. Boy was I wrong. I first began to realize just how wrong when the green face of some alien being appeared on the screen mouthing the words, "Ah! An opponent for my enjoyment. Get ready to do battle."

Suddenly the screen was filled with vicious space attackers all converging on my tiny space ship. While I was trying to decide whether I was supposed to push the thruster to shoot or the shooter to thrust one of them annihilated me.

Then it was Fred's turn. Quicker than I can describe it he was spinning his space ship around, dancing back and forth, deftly maneuvering it out of harm's way and picking off attackers right and left. As soon as he had cleaned out one bunch the machine racked up several thousand bonus points and turned loose another flock of attackers. Same thing, only that time he was shooting out the sides and back of his space ship at the same time.

"Mine didn't do that," I complained.

"All in knowing how, Dad," he said, as he once again zapped the screen clear.

Finally, after about five minutes he could see I was getting a bit bored so he decided to sacrifice his space ship to give me another turn. That time I actually got one attacker before the other 11 got me. Whoopee.

I could almost hear those aliens laughing—or maybe it was Fred. Sometimes it's hard to tell the difference. Mercifully the game finally came to an end. Never in all my years have I ever been so totally demolished. When the machine tallied up I had 16 points. Fred had somewhere around 1,763,000.

But then came the crowning blow. That disgusting green face came back on the screen and started mouthing words again. "You," it smirked, "were an amusing opponent."

Amusing? I didn't see anything funny about it. Inept, maybe but not amusing. Fred, however, seemed to enjoy it. The sickly green face called him an "outstanding" opponent.

I had to admit the green face was half right.

Due to Technical Difficulties….

It all started when we bought a VCR. I carefully read the instruction book even though it appeared to have lost something in the translation from Japanese to English. With a little help from my son, Fred, who understands these things, I finally got to the place where I was ready to try a recording session.

One of the television stations was showing "The Hindenburg" as its midnight movie. Since I had missed it when it played the theaters a few years back I selected it as my first effort.

An evening or two later, Mrs. H and I sat down to view it. Great movie. George C. Scott was superb. Tension was building as the huge airship droned across the Atlantic. A plot to destroy it was unfolding right before our eyes. Someone planted an incendiary device, timed to go off after the dirigible landed, in the girders. The idea was to disrupt German-American relations or embarrass the Nazi party or something like that.

But as the airship neared New Jersey, fog and rain moved in unexpectedly, delaying the landing. It became obvious that the ship was heading for a mid-air disaster. About that time, just as the huge airship disappeared into a fog bank, the television screen went white.

Now Mrs. H, who is not particularly well versed in electrical matters, immediately jumped to the unwarranted conclusion that I had set the VCR incorrectly so that it quit recording before the movie ended. I, of course, carefully explained to her that the people who made the movie did so for the purpose of telling he real story of the Hindenburg. I explained that, rather than exploding and burning at the Lakehurst terminal—as was widely reported at the time—the airship was really lost in a sudden snowstorm.

"That's how the movie ended," I said.

I don't think she bought that story, but being an understanding woman, after a day or two she quit jawing me about it. Not long after that we were munching popcorn and watching a tape I'd made of the Forrest Tucker movie, "Rock Island Line." About an hour into it, just about the time the bad guys were getting ready to ambush the good guys on the train, that movie also came to an abrupt end.

I quickly explained that "Rock Island Line" was one of those old-time serials they used to run for kids on Saturday afternoons. All we had to do I said was to wait until next week and they'd be showing the rest.

"That's twice," she said.

Now, a couple weeks ago, we were watching my tape of "Big Country." Gregory Peck had just whupped a bad ranch foreman who was jealous of Peck for becoming engaged to a girl the foreman thought was his private property. A few minutes later, Peck discovered another fine example of womanhood in the neighborhood and began to admire the scenery over that way. That's when the screen went white.

"Dust storm," I called out.

Believe me, friends, Mrs. H didn't buy that explanation one bit. "Dust storm, my eye," she said. "You blew it again." I think she said some other things, too but events were moving so rapidly about then that I can't remember.

Now the scene changes. First let me say, Mrs. H is not one to hold a grudge. She's more inclined to get even. It was a week or two later. I was sitting on the sofa with one eye on the evening paper and the other on Dan Rather. Out of the corner of the newspaper eye, I saw her coming with a white shirt in her hand.

This she spread out before me. There was a fairly obvious lipstick smudge near the collar.

Even though her toe was tapping, her voice was all sweetness as she said, "This is your shirt, is it not?"

I am a dead man. Innocent until proven guilty? Not in this court. Hoping desperately to buy a little time I said the only thing I could say, considering the circumstances: "Well it looks like my shirt."

"Can you explain this smudge?"

"No, your honor, I can't."

"Do you want to try and explain this smudge?"

"No, your honor, I don't."

"Why not?"

"Because I can't, your honor."

Then I noticed a twinkle in her eye. The twinkle was followed by a chuckle. I nervously joined in. Then came the laughter. Gales of laughter. Tears running down her cheeks. She was almost rolling on the floor.

"Gotcha," she said. "Gotcha, and you had it coming for messing up those VCR movies and then trying to alibi yourself out with those cock-and-bull stories. I put that smudge on there myself"

Glory be! Hallelujah! The sun is shining! The governor's office just called with a reprieve! I'll live to hang another day! But can anyone tell me which girl Gregory Peck finally ended up marrying?

Lew Hudson

Solving Bridgit's Problems Doesn't Clear Slate

"How do you expect to fix a dishwasher when you can't program a VCR?" That was a low blow. I admit I've had problems with the VCR, but it isn't my fault. VCRs have a mind of their own and mine doesn't like me.

"What," I said to Mrs. H, "does programming a VCR have to do with fixing a dishwasher?" Bridgit, our dishwasher, has been ailing. The instruction book said to hang that little container of chemical that prevents water spots in the upper left-hand corner. Water, however wasn't getting to it.

My first suggestion was to do nothing. Most machines fix themselves when they learn that sulking won't get them any special attention. That didn't help.

"Maybe you should avoid putting dishes in that area so as to leave a clear path for the water to reach the chemical," I said. That didn't work either.

Then it occurred to me that maybe the little whirligig that sprays water upward might be stuck. She checked and it wasn't. About that time I was fresh out of ideas. "I guess I'm going to have to take a look at it," I said. "I'll do it just as soon as I have time."

That's when it happened. "What good would that do?" she said. "You don't know anything about dishwashers."

"Shsssssh," I said. "Bridgit will hear you. She doesn't know I don't know. Maybe I can bluff her." And that's when she delivered the coup de grace about my record as VCR programmer.

It was a cheap shot, but I didn't let that deter me. Males have roles to play in this world. Looking studiously into the workings of machinery is one of them.

After supper the other evening I rolled up my sleeves and grabbed a flashlight. "What are you going to do?" she asked.

"I'm going to fix Bridgit," I replied. I didn't quite hear what she said under her breath as she turned to go into the living rom. It's probably just as well. The little whirligig is the source of the water that's supposed to hit the container of anti-spot chemical so I figured that was the place to start.

I looked in one end. Clear as a bell. Spinning it around I shined the light in the other. Bingo! It was plugged. A little deft work with a turkey skewer fished it out.

"There she is," I said with a smile as I handed Mrs. H a little chip from the edge of a dish. I could see she was impressed. "Thanks," she said. "But you still can't program a VCR.

You Have to Show a Car Who's the Boss

Unless I'm going out of town I never put more than $5 worth of gas in my car. Mrs. H wonders why I don't fill 'er up. I tell her you can't wean a car with a full gas tank.

My car gets 32 miles to the gallon. Hers gets 28. She claims that's because hers is a V-6 and mine a four. I tell her that's got nothing to do with it. It's a matter of discipline.

Just ask any old Navy man. Let a car get the upper hand and it's trouble every time. I made that mistake once with an Audi and paid dearly. That car rewarded my good nature by coughing up her distributor in Friday afternoon rush hour traffic on the freeway in downtown Fort Worth.

There wasn't any reason for it other than a streak of cussed independence. Over the next few months she broke an accelerator cable in Minneapolis, a motor mount in the middle of nowhere in Iowa and an electric fuel pump miles from anywhere on a southwestern Minnesota prairie.

That did it. I walked away and never looked back. The first garage I came to I traded her sight unseen for a Buick and told the guy to go out and drag her useless carcass to town.

Give a car an inch and it'll take the whole yardstick.

I had to remind Jezebel, my Oldsmobile, of that the other day. Remember that 20 below day back before Christmas? Jezebel figured that was a good morning to test me. When I went out to go to work she wouldn't so much as belch.

I could have humored her, I suppose by plugging in the block heater to warm her innards but that would only have encouraged her. Instead I got out, slammed her door, kicked her left front tire and borrowed Mrs. H's car for the day. By evening she was more docile. You've got to be tough. If cars want to play hard ball then that's the game for you.

Mrs. H doesn't see it that way. She's gentle. She loves her car. It loves her. For her it purrs. For me it growls and I growl back.

If her car was mine I'd cut her gas ration to $3. She'd gasp before she'd get another drink. I never pass up a chance to tell Jezebel how nice she's got it. I remind her of the new tires I bought her last summer and the oil change I treated her to in October.

Heh, Jezebel, don't give me any of that "too cold to start" routine. Remember: I can always sell you to a teenager.

A Few Easy Steps for Fixing the Car

A fellow gets lots of advice when something goes wrong with the car. This time it was the turn signals. They quit blinking. When I pulled the lever the little green arrow on the dash came on and stayed on.

"Better get that fixed," she said, "before we leave for Slayton on Friday."

That was Saturday a week ago. I didn't respond for a couple of reasons. First, replacing anything on an automobile costs money. Second, rash decisions that cost me money are against my principals.

I knew she wouldn't be sympathetic to the first, because it was my car and my checkbook. I wasn't sure I could adequately explain the second, so I just kept quiet.

I've developed a system for dealing with malfunctioning car accessories. When something quits, sit down and think about it. Take a little time. Choose a good spot. One of the best thinking places is a recliner. It helps to close the eyes. Better yet, sleep on it. Two or three nights is a good beginning.

There's always time for Step Two—the old Hindu approach to car trouble—bangladesh. If one bang doesn't do it, don't be afraid to try two or three at different places.

There are dangers of course. Vigorous bangladesh, although it sometimes revives the faulty part, can cause other parts to malfunction. If that happens, just keep the technique to yourself.

That failing, you can move on to Step Three—poking around. Automobile poking is fairly safe, because the highest voltage likely to be encountered, unless you have the misfortune to short out a capacitor, is 12. Poking it is not recommended where 110 volts are running around loose.

Even so, it should be done properly. In the case of turn signals, whose mechanisms are always behind the dash, it is expedient to remove your eyeglasses. Otherwise you'll bend 'em for sure, trying to reach around the steering wheel. Besides, bifocals aren't worth a hoot for looking upward.

Removing them shows off your thoughtful look to best advantage and enhances your reputation as an expert. An occasional "hmmmmmmmm"or "aaagghhh" helps.

"Well, that ought to do it," I said.

"But aren't you going to test then?" she asked. "We need turn signals when we go down to Slayton."

"No point in that," I said. "They'll either work or they won't. No point spending any more time on 'em."

The situation was critical. I had about a 10 percent chance the poking around had reconnected a loose wire or separated a couple that were shorted out.

If the signals worked the next day, my reputation was intact. If not, I could always take the car to the garage and pay whatever they asked. I lucked out. Next morning the signals came unstuck all by themselves.

"All in knowing how," I told her cheerfully.

"My hero," she replied.

Only she wasn't smiling.

Dispatches From Our Corner of the Globe

Communicating with a Talking Post is Rough Duty

Don't blame me if posts can't talk plain. It happened a while back. Mrs. H and I were out for an evening drive. The weather was hot. It was a perfect time for an ice cream cone. Mrs. H suggested we pull into one of the local fast food places. "You won't even have to get out of the car," she said.

How it got to be my job to get out and go get the food is something I've never understood. Someday I'll have to talk about that. For now, we're talking about talking posts.

Not having to get out sounded good. The car air conditioner was working fine. The only problem was the post. I don't mind talking into a telephone and before I was a newspaper writer I was a broadcaster so I'm comfortable around microphones. I don't have any communication hang-ups.

Except for posts. Talking to a post in the drive-through lane of a fast-food restaurant seems to me a particularly demeaning thing to do. If I ran a fast food restaurant I'd set up a mannequin with a microphone in her belly button next to the menu board. But they don't do that. Instead they hang a microphone and loud speaker on a wooden post and expect people to spill their guts.

So I was already in a foul mood when I pulled up to the post to place our order. It didn't help that the post was on my side of the car. That's another bone I have to pick. Who decreed that drivers have to do all the post talking? What's wrong with a post on the passenger side?

The menu board listed about 103 choices, including four flavors of ice cream and three different cone sizes in either soft or old fashioned ice cream.

Given a choice between modern and old fashioned my knee jerk reaction invariably is old fashioned, but that evening soft ice cream sounded better so I told the post, "Two large vanilla soft ice cream cones please."

I thought that was clear enough even though I felt silly with my head out the car window talking to a post. But then the post talked back.

Why restaurant owners assign people with their harshest voices to post duty is something I don't understand. This lady had a voice that could score glass.

"Fraschel breet nashtawfu shoots," she said.

"Huh?" I said.

She must have not understood the flavor. "Vanilla," I told her. "Two vanilla."

There was laughter from the other side of the car. "What she said," Mrs. H explained, "was for you to have $1.59 ready when you get to the window."

"Then why didn't she just say so," I grumbled.

I paid the bill and got our cones., I ate mine in silence. By the time I was through my mind was made up. Next time I have occasion to talk to a post I'm going to say, "Pflunz the falatarapp. Two ratzifritz with bluncheroo on the arpichum."

I can't wait to see what it says to that.

Machines Have Minds of Their Own

Somehow or other we weren't surprised. We were in the midst of a large washing and the machine was filled to the brim when suddenly the lights dimmed and the motor quit. "Overload," I said.

Mrs. H was somewhat more succinct. What do you do with a washerful of soggy clothes? In the old days it would have been simple. We would have run them through a wringer and hung them on a line.

No one does things like that anymore. Equipment failures paralyze us. A few years ago a multiple equipment failure blacked out the whole Eastern seaboard. News reports said life came to a standstill.

To be held hostage by your equipment is bad enough but when you consider that equipment has minds of its own the prospects are frightening. So for some diabolical reason it picks the worst possible times to go belly up.

Freezers, for example. Did you ever hear of one failing in January? No way. The months for freezer failure are July and August.

Clothes dryers pick rainy days. They never quit when the sun is shining. Cars are even worse. We were driving through downtown

Fort Worth at 4 p.m. on Friday afternoon when the distributor vomited parts all over the engine compartment.

Luckily we had enough momentum to coast down an exit ramp into the parking lot of a convenience store. Had it not been for a mechanic with a heart we would have spent the weekend in a motel and who knows how much money.

I know inanimate objects aren't supposed to have minds of their own but you just haven't met our water pump. Since Southdale got city water a few years ago it has faithfully delivered well water to our outside faucets.

One evening a couple weeks ago I made the mistake of touching the pressure gauge that promptly fell off, releasing a 35-pound stream of water.

I stemmed the tide with my finger like that Dutch boy at the dike and yelled for Mrs. H. We got the pump shut down, the pressure released, and the hole temporarily plugged. It was after hours of course. It always is.

When the washer had that spell of sciatica we left it until the following day and called a serviceman. You guessed it. When he came it worked perfectly. When he left he suggested we spend some time shopping for a new washer.

Over in the corner I swear the washer was chuckling. Now all I have to worry about is the bill.

Outmoded Slide Rule Still Computes

It had been years since I had seen it—my old high school slide rule—but there it was tucked away in the back of a desk drawer. I picked it up. My mind raced back to the pre-computer age when the most sophisticated computing machine in our town was a hand operated adding machine at the bank.

The idea of an electronic device capable of instantaneously solving complex mathematical problems hadn't yet crossed anyone's mind. That such devices might be made small enough to fit in a shirt pocket was beyond comprehension. That they could be made and sold for $8 or $10 was ludicrous. That they could be operated on the power of light was ridiculous.

To those of us accustomed to laboriously working problems with pencil and paper, slide rules were remarkable devices. They were to my generation what pocket calculators are for students of today.

I doubt they even make them anymore. They obviously would be no match for sophisticated pocket calculators but they were head and shoulders above the way we had been doing math.

Our math teacher was afraid slide rules would make things too simple. She imposed a firm regulation that every student had to know the mathematical formula for a problem before being allowed to solve it with the slide rule.

To us they were amazing devices capable of rapidly doing multiplication and division, extracting square and cube roots, solving proportions and calculating sines, cosines, tangents and logarithms.

They still are, although that old requirement of first having to know the formula before being able to use the slide rule to solve it severely limits me now. The instruction pamphlet was folded up inside the case. I got it out and spent a couple fascinating hours refreshing my memory before trying a few calculations.

Age hasn't hurt it at all. The old slide rule still works. Answers it produced agreed exactly with my pocket calculator.

Dispatches From Our Corner of the Globe

Reach Out...and Touch a Computer

She started laughing even before she hung up the telephone.

"What," I asked, "is so funny?"

"I just had a crazy idea," she said.

I was not surprised. Crazy ideas are not unheard of with Mrs. H. "That telephone call gave you a crazy idea?" I said.

"Yes. It was one of those computerized voices telling me my order had arrived and I could go out and pick it up."

That didn't seem particularly hilarious to me so I pushed for further information. "So why is that so funny?"

"It's not the call," she said. "It's just a thought that crossed my mind while the computer was talking. What do you suppose happens when a computerized telephone calling machine calls one of those computerized telephone answering machines? What do they say to one another?"

I saw the point. We both started laughing. It has all sorts of interesting possibilities—"Hello, this is a recorded message from J.C. Roeward telling....Hi, this is Lonnie Yuppie speaking. I'm not home...your order...right now if you'll leave...is ready to be picked...your name and number...up at...after the tone...our store anytime...I'll get back...during regular business...to you...hours."

With any luck at all, we decided, the two disembodied artificial voices might keep on trying to communicate with one another till kingdom come and leave us humans alone.

Case of the Balky Toaster

That old law that forever action there is an equal and opposite reaction was never more true than in the case of the toaster with a mind of its own. The story started when Mrs. H and I were newlyweds. Few people have set up housekeeping with less.

When we moved to our first home, a furnished apartment, all our earthly possessions fitted nicely into the trunk and one corner of the back seat of a 1948 Plymouth sedan.

Today brides get more loot at a shower than we got at our wedding. One present, though, was a state-of-the-art 1950 model toaster—post-war technology at its best.

All you had to do was place the bread in the slots. That triggered a little switch and the bread was slowly lowered into the innards. Once there, according to the book, the device took a reading on the color of the bread, analyzed its moisture content and scheduled the amount of toasting time needed to produce a golden brown hue every time.

It worked. Every morning for almost 30 years it produced perfect toast. Nothing else we owned worked as well.

As a result, mornings were tranquil, unmarked by marital tension. Then, as in the case of the wonderful, one horse shay described by Oliver Wendell Holmes, that old friend came to the end of its useful life.

It didn't malfunction. It simply quit. Analysis showed an irreparable break in the heating element. "Don't worry," I said bravely. "They still make 'em. We'll just go down to the appliance store and buy a new one."

Friends, they don't make 'em like they used to. To be sure, current models look like the 1950 version but that's where similarity ends. Innards are decidedly different.

From that day on, mornings lost their tranquility around the Hudson house. The first replacement lasted two weeks before it, too developed an irreparable heating element break. The second, while still intact, has become the bane of our existence.

For no reason whatsoever, it develops spells when it won't lower bread into the furnace room. Now Mrs. H isn't one of the people who hate mornings. In fact, she almost enjoys them. Normally she can handle getting up and fixing breakfast. All she asks is that the machinery cooperates.

When it doesn't—when the percolator boils over or the toaster starts playing games—her fuse is pretty short. In recent years I've lost track of the number of mornings I have awakened to the sound of a female hand repeatedly slamming slices of bread into the toaster—each slam progressively harder—each muttered comment louder.

Discretion being the better part of valor, I quietly turn over, pull the blankets over my ears and pretend to go back to sleep.

It doesn't work, though. Sooner or later it's time to get up and face discordant music. One morning, after a particularly frustrating session, she suggested that I hold the toaster while she kicked it over the jack pines into the next county.

I didn't fall for that. She wouldn't guarantee her aim. Another time she suggested that I plan on looking for the toaster in a backyard snow drift. Generally, I just keep quiet.

It's not that I'm not sympathetic. On mornings when it's my turn to fix breakfast, the toaster occasionally acts up too, but I just keep slamming until it learns who's boss.

The problem is cost. Our first toaster probably set someone

back $10 or so. At 30 cents or so a year, it was a good investment. This one cost more than $50. It won't be amortized until about 1995.

Mrs. H doesn't see it that way. If I'd agree she'd blow our life savings searching for one that works. One day at an auction I had to restrain her from bidding on one of those folding campfire toasters you see in the outdoor catalogs.

"Those things never work," I said.

"Neither does—oh never mind,"

Lew Hudson

Chapter 9

Uninvited Guests

Mr. and Mrs. H have always graciously opened their home to guests of all kinds. Family, friends, acquaintance and strangers alike, all have been welcome at the Hudson home. Indeed Mom and Dad are most happy when their rooms are filled with laughter and good cheer. Good times are had by all, memories made and cherished. But there are a few guests that they refuse to welcome warmly into the fold. Through the years Dad regaled his readers with the saga of Claude and Maude, resident squirrels at their Baxter home. The swashbuckling tales of his efforts to outwit the rodents never failed to delight and amuse.

Lew Hudson

Why Try to Fool the Squirrels?

I surrender. They beat me. I've taken down my squirrel shields. From now on squirrels are welcome at the bird feeder.

It's not that I didn't try. For a while I even thought I might win. After all, what chance does a squirrel have against the cunning intellect of a man?

A big chance, I was to learn.

The struggle started when we put up a bird feeder. Because we like to watch the birds, we hung it from the eave outside the window of our family room. "If I hang it back from the edge," I told Mrs. H, "the squirrels won't be able to reach it."

For a moment or two after I said that I thought I heard laughter in the trees, but I figured it was just the wind rubbing two branches together.

So I hung the feeder. A couple hours later the first chickadee sampled a sunflower seed or two. About 15 minutes after that a fat squirrel had climbed up there and was gorging himself.

Out the door I stormed with a piece of galvanized sheet metal and some wood screws. "I'll just line the eave with metal," I told Mrs. H. "That way, they won't be able to hang on when they come over the roof."

I was wrong. The barrier was too short. Next day I put on an extension.

"There's no way they can make it now," I told her cheerfully. I was half right. The metal barred their way from the roof. So they climbed up the side of the house.

"Don't worry," I told Mrs. H. "I've just begun to fight."

I got some old aluminum press plates from the guys in the pressroom and sheathed the side of the house with a slick metal barrier. That evening I looked up from the evening paper. There was a real blimp
of a squirrel gorging on the sunflower seeds.

"They're back," Mrs. H said.

"More metal," I replied.

This time I put up barriers from every direction. "I've got 'em this time," I chortled.

Calling Mrs. H to the window I said, "Look." Three or four squirrels on the ground were eying the bird feeder and talking among themselves.

One hopped upon the side of the house and gingerly tried to sink a claw where the metal started. He jumped down. I laughed out loud. "They're stumped," I said.

Another tried to come over the edge of the roof and almost lost his footing. "I win," I said. "No squirrel can beat me when I set my mind to it."

Mrs. H was uncharacteristically quiet. I sensed a certain lack of confidence. All she said was, "that metal looks a little strange."

"Don't worry," I replied. "I'll paint it so it'll match the siding."

I slept like a baby that night and went off to work the next morning, chuckling to myself. That evening there wasn't a squirrel in sight.

But I noticed a couple of things I hadn't seen before. In two or three places the siding was splintered. "I never noticed our siding was in such tough shape," I said to Mrs. H.

The next day it had deteriorated more. Siding was splintered in a dozen or more places. And then I saw something else. In two places the metal sheathing was gnawed away. I showed it to Mrs. H.

"That's it," she said. "You made them mad and now they're starting to eat our house. You've got to surrender while we can still keep out the rain."

It was a tough decision. Surrender? Me? Surrender to a bunch of squirrels?

"Do you remember what the American commander told the Germans when they demanded surrender in the Battle of the Bulge in World War II?" I asked.

"No," she said. "Tell me."

"'Nuts'. That's what he said. 'Nuts'."

She was quiet for a moment. "And you want to say that to a bunch of squirrels?:

I saw her point. I got out the stepladder, took down every piece of metal sheathing from the battered wall and sadly carried the bird feeder to the garage.

"When I get around to it," I said, "I'll hang it in the tree."

"Maybe you could put a metal shield on it to keep the squirrels off," she said.

"No," I replied. "they'd just cut down the tree."

Lew Hudson

More on the Squirrel Battle

Now about those squirrels. Our three daughters were home for Thanksgiving, vowing to take up the squirrel struggle I had abandoned the week before.

"Forget it," I said. "I'm a beaten man."

"Nonsense," they declared. "We'll figure a way to keep them out of the bird feeder."

"You mean the squirrel feeder," I said.

They acted as if they didn't hear me. Out to the tree they went with the untempered optimism of youth. I stayed inside. I know when I'm beat.

Their first effort was to string a rope between two trees and suspend the feeder from it. I almost laughed out loud. There was no way that was going to fool the squirrels. It didn't.

"We'll get 'em Dad," they said.

Off to the store they went and came home with a plastic squirrel baffle.

"This'll do it," they said. "It says so right here on the label."

I looked. It did. "Squirrel baffle?" I asked. "That's a contradiction in terms."

They just ignored me and went gaily out to the tree to install their purchase. The squirrels stepped back for a moment to let them work.

Over the next couple hours I observed that about 12 percent of the squirrel population in our neighborhood is dumb. The other 88 percent went past that baffle like a freight train passing a tramp.

Mrs. H was fit to be tied. I haven't seen that look in her eye for years. As a precaution, I kept a watchful eye on the gun closet and hid the ammunition.

"I can't believe it," our oldest daughter said as she watched the bushy bandits gorge themselves on expensive sunflower seeds.

"I can," I said.

But even I was surprised at what happened next. I had been busy for a couple hours and wasn't paying any attention to what was happening outside. Just before dark, however, I looked out toward the oak tree. The squirrel feeder was gone.

The rope was still there. So were the hook and the squirrel baffle, but the feeder itself was gone.

Then I looked toward the ground. There it was—one corner sticking out of a snow bank. A couple of squirrels were lolling alongside. I swear I heard one belch.

Now I suppose you're going to tell me squirrels don't have wrenches and screwdrivers with which to unfasten brackets and the like. Our daughters tried that line on me too. I just laughed.

Our oldest daughter slowly made her way to the tree, picked up the feeder and brought it to the house. I noticed her shoulders were a little stooped—like mine were two weeks ago when the squirrels defeated me.

The feeder is in the garage now, behind locked doors. Our daughters are back in their homes—older and wiser. The squirrels are back in their trees, dieting.

And Mrs. H is talking assassination.

Dispatches From Our Corner of the Globe

Requiem for a Tree Frog

From time to time I've been accused of harboring excessive animosity toward some of the wild creatures with whom we share life with on Ashdale Lane in Baxter.

It is true. I have tried diabolical schemes to frustrate squirrels at the bird feeder, and I have written unkind words about robins singing off key at 4:30 a.m. But the record should show that I am not alone in this.

There's a lady living at the same address who also has an aversion to close proximity with certain types of living creatures. The family lives in awe of her reaction when snakes have approached the house or gophers invaded her flower beds.

Even so, I was surprised the other day when the tree frogs turned up missing. We've had a pair living on the deck since spring, when they mistook the umbrella for a tree.

Although they are harmless, pretty creatures, they did leave traces of their presence on the table and several times startled us by sudden leaps. Even so, I wasn't prepared for what happened. One evening I raised the umbrella and they were gone.

"What happened to the frogs?" I asked.

"They're gone," she said.

"Gone?" I said. "Gone as in a one-way journey to that big frog pond in the sky?"

She hesitated, choosing her words carefully before replying.

"Let's just say they croaked."

Animals Poised to Retaliate

I didn't intend to start a fight. All I wanted was to clear some rotten wood from the core of a sick oak in our front yard.

The tree apparently was damaged years ago and, although still alive, has long suffered from decay. I figured if I trimmed out the rotten stuff with my chainsaw, it might help the tree heal and get on with the job of providing shade and shelter.

So I did, but you'd have thought I'd declared war. A colony of carpenter ants lived in there. They swarmed out by the thousands—some carrying eggs, others bits of food and still others just trying to bite a chunk out of whomever was responsible for the turmoil.

I ignored their protests, did what I had set out to do and retired to the house. That was all there was to it, or so I thought.

Next day however, I was in the yard doing some scientific research into the cooling power of southwesterly breezes. I told Mrs. H it was better to be doing something worthwhile than just loafing.

Suddenly, out of the corner of my eye, I spotted something under a small ornamental evergreen. Stooping down, I saw what appeared to be a bunch of ants marching along—in step.

Off to one side was a solitary fellow who, as near as I could tell without getting too close, was wearing a campaign hat and a Sam Brown belt. Now, my hearing isn't what it used to be, but I swear a small voice was yelling, "Hup two, three, four."

And they were singing—a catchy tune—something about marching two by two. I don't mind telling you, that shook me up. The light wasn't very good but it looked like the ants were wearing little steel helmets. They were carrying things too.

It was not a pretty sight.

But that wasn't all. Behind a jack pine was our pet squirrel, Claude—the scourge of the bird feeder. Claude had his head down to the ground as if conferring with someone pretty small.

And, on a low branch above Claude's head, sat Batman, the biggest, fattest, nastiest robin in the neighborhood. He also appeared engrossed in the conversation.

"You don't suppose...." Mrs. H asked.

"Yep," I said. "It looks like they've formed an animal Axis and declared war."

That's something we've long feared. Humans are supposed to subdue the world and make it productive. It seems to have worked about everywhere except on Ashdale Lane in Baxter. There the squirrels gorge on bird seed. There the robins commit unmentionable indiscretions.   And now the ants were marching.

I remember that old song the Girl Scouts used to sing when I was a Brownie Daddy. It went, "The ants go marching two by two, hoorah, hoorah."

I always considered it a fun song. Little did I know it would one day be used to whip attack troops into an emotional frenzy.

"Where will it come?" I asked Mrs. H. "Front door? Back door? The windows?"

"There, there," she said. "I think we're ready. I've put a fly swatter at each door. I'm keeping a kettle of hot water on the stove and if all else fails, there's....there's the bomb."

"The bomb?" I said. "The big one?" The bug bomb itself?"

"Yes," she said. "We'll do what we have to do. We'll fight 'em in the entryway. We'll fight 'em in the kitchen. We'll fight 'em in the bath. We'll fight 'em in the bedroom"....Her voice trailed off.

Suddenly I felt a little better.

Batman and Robin to the Rescue

One of us came unglued.

Not without good cause, I might add. A bat flying through the house can do that to a person.

Faced with bats in the belfry, people don't always act rationally. They break out in goosebumps, they duck, cover their heads, cower in corners and are about as useful as the teats on a boar.

When that bat swooped into our living room the other evening, a certain amount of fear was understandable. Fortunately, one of us kept a cool head.

"Pull yourself together," Mrs. H said sharply. "What are we going to do about it?"

I didn't have the foggiest notion. I had never faced a bat before. Mad dogs, black bears, timber wolves and door-to-door salesmen, yes—but bats, no.

"Maybe you could catch it in my landing net," I suggested hopefully.

"Won't work," she said. "The mesh is too large."

"I'll call my friend Lowell Rosnau," I said. "Maybe he'll have an idea.

So I did and he did. "Get a tennis racket," he said, "and activate your smoke alarm. The squeal disorients them so they fly around in circles and you can whack 'em."

There are times when a man has to faced his limitations. This was one of them.

"Will you come over and help me?" I asked.

"In a little while," he said.

Those are four of the nicest words in the English language. While we were waiting, Mrs. H shooed the thing into the bedroom and closed the door. I would have helped if my knees hadn't turned to jelly.

When Lowell and Dottie arrived with a couple rackets I meekly volunteered to help. Dottie looked me over, thought a moment and then said she and Lowell usually work as a team.

"Batman and Robin?" I quipped.

It was one of the shortest badminton games on record. One squeal from the smoke detector, a mighty whomp from a racket and it was all over.

Lowell came out of the bedroom carrying the invader. "What do you want done with him?" he asked.

"Outside," I said, "and I want him very dead."

Friends like the Rosnaus are invaluable in emergencies.

Men like me are not

This War with Squirrels Is No New Development

Sooner or later I figured Larry Batson would get back to the squirrels. The last time he wrote about their inhumanity was in 1980 when he was doing a column for the Minneapolis Tribune.

Now that he's retired, Batson did a longer piece on the same subject for the winter edition of Bond, the Lutheran Brotherhood magazine.

Batson entitled it, "Squirrels: 1000 Humans: 1."

I wasn't aware we ever scored a victory, but Batson said he once foiled a squirrel named Fat Bandit by coating the bird feeder pole with motor oil additive STP.

Batson, like Hudson, grew up in squirrel country. He came from the Ozarks and I from Davis County, Iowa, the foothills of the Ozarks. Down that way people love squirrels. Opening day of the hunting season is one of the year's major holidays.

At our house we particularly love 'em fried and simmered for a half hour or so in brown gravy and onions. It's the natural order of things. Squirrels are supposed to feed humans, not the other way around.

"Did Andy Jackson feed squirrels?" Batson asks rhetorically. Certainly not. He ate 'em and won the battle of New Orleans.

It's still going on. I saw Claude and Maude the other day and they looked a little haggard. Claude didn't have the energy to shinny more than five or six feet up the bird feeder pole and Maude just scavenged up what few crumbs she could find on the ground.

If I didn't know better, I'd swear he was ailing. Claude, however, isn't the ailing kind. I think he's worried about the nephews.

Herman, Sherman and Vermin haven't been around since before Christmas and the last time we saw Thurman was around New Year's.

I blame it on my neighbor's live trap. All winter, Darrell's been escorting them to the edge of town with firm instructions not to look back until they get to Pillager.

Whether that's the reason or whether failure of the acorn crop last fall is to blame is a moot question. The fact is squirrel tracks are becoming scarce. Maybe Darrell ought to ease up. A neighborhood without squirrels isn't nearly as fun.

Claude and Maude, You Are Missed in Baxter

How can I say this? It's beginning to look like Claude and Maude have gone to that big oak tree in the sky.

Claude and Maude are the progenitors of Baxter's best known squirrel family.

Considering the nasty things I've written about them over the years, you might think their apparent demise is cause for rejoicing, but you'd be wrong. To be sure, Claude and Maude were something less than ideal neighbors. In the years I've lived with them they've shown absolutely no respect.

Claude has never passed an opportunity to thumb his nose at me. Maude is no better. Together they reared one of the rottenest rodent families in Crow Wing County history. With their nephews Herman, Sherman, Thurman, and Vermin, they've made life miserable. But that's no cause to celebrate their apparent long-term departure.

We journalists aren't cut out that way. No matter how reprehensible the subjects about which we write, we don't let it get personal.

O. Henry used to write about the charming rogues and thieves he encountered. I've run into a few likeable con men myself. Most journalists secretly admire the politicians about which they write. Every murderer I've known was interesting. Interesting.

If, in fact, Claude and Maude are gone, we're going to miss them. His white ears and pot belly were a familiar sight around the yard. And Maude's harried look—the result of living with Claude—always evoked sympathy.

They were getting old, but the last time I saw them they were anything but malnourished. Their nephews saw to that. They routinely scattered more seeds than they ate.

That's why I know the old folks didn't starve. I'm more inclined to think they got staved.

A lot of squirrels out our way have been. Other than the time he spent harassing seagulls in Florida last winter, my neighbor Darrel Stave has been trapping squirrels and escorting them to the edge of town with a stern warning not to look back.

Warnings are not likely to have awed Claude and Maude, but they're getting a little long in the tooth. Their eyes aren't what they used to be. Their feet hurt. They might not have been able to walk all the way back.

I have a reputation to uphold, so I can't say this to just everyone, but the fact is, we're going to miss them.

Life without Claude and Maude just won't be the same.

Better, maybe, but not nearly as much fun.

A Final Note....

The occasion came in 1990 when our father was hospitalized with a heart attack that the Hudson kids collectively wrote Dad's column that week. We saw this as an opportunity to resurrect a few old stories, some of which Dad might have preferred to let rest peacefully. We also saw this as a chance to repay our dear father for the quips he had so lovingly made about each of us in his column.

LuAnn

One of our earliest entertainment was our evening drives along the gravel roads of southwestern Minnesota. We jumped into the car after supper and toured the countryside. If we were really lucky —and Mom was hungry—we stopped for a root beer or Dilly Bar. Or Dad brought his rifle and did a little pheasant hunting while we waited in the car. After many of Dad's unsuccessful hunting outings, Cindy and I carefully drew a pheasant picture and gave it to him for reference.

Mom and Dad were always adopting people—mainly kids who needed a little attention—such as the young couple that showed up at our table one Thanksgiving. They turned out to be friends of my sister and had been unable to get to the relative's house because of bad weather. At least for that Thanksgiving they had plenty of relatives, all named Hudson.

Cindy

No one looks forward to Halloween more than my father. By the end of September, his eyes take on a fiendish gleam as he plots tricks on his victims. His favorite target used to be our neighbor, Charles "Chuckles" Moore who lived a few houses from us. Naturally we became his willing accomplices. One year he sent us to Chuckle's house to distract him. We chatted indoors while Dad carefully laid out a grave, complete with tombstone outside.

The following year Dad was in even finer form. He tied fishing line across the street, softly banging the door until good old Chuckles came out to investigate, only to find no one was there.
Some Halloweens Dad sent us to carry out dastardly deeds. One time he assembled us kids and a couple of friends, passed out toilet paper and instructed us not to come back until we had emptied our rolls at the Williams' house.

Another year while we were all out tormenting victims, our own backyard was tp'd. It looked like the Cypress Gardens. Dad took it in stride and sent Mom out with empty toilet paper rolls to gather up the remains. "Waste not, want not," he always says.

Becky

When I was a child, my dad was a constant source of counseling, guidance and concern. When nobody else seemed to care, Dad always knew when something was amiss with me. He managed to force the troubles out of me in heart-to-heart talks, whether I wanted to talk or not, and knew the words that would make me feel better. For that I thank you, Dad.

Dad has always prided himself on doing things himself. Imagine his delight when he dismantled and reassembled a Volkswagen with only one or two pieces left over. It was my first automobile and I cherished it even though it was not beautiful and had to be towed home. For weeks Dad stationed himself in the garage, studying his Volkswagen manual and piecing the car back together.

I will never forget the day he took me out for my first driving lesson in that car. He patiently described the workings of a clutch automobile and turned me loose. When I began rolling backwards at the stop sign on the hill he only grimaced quietly.

After that 1965 Volkswagen had taken me many miles—and two weeks after Dad had repainted it—a pickup truck backed into it downtown. I angrily jumped out and yelled at the offender, "Hey! What are doing? It would not have been so bad but my dad just painted this car!!" am I proud of Dad? You bet. He has always given us his very best.

Fred

We were exploring an old settler's cabin in northern Minnesota one summer day. Dad said he would go ahead and make sure there weren't any wild animals. As he crept cautiously forward, Mom picked up a long branch and poked him in the backside. Without looking around Dad said, "Just a minute, Fred." No one said anything. Mom poked him again. Same response. After the fourth poke Dad looked around in exasperation, ready to give it to me for disobeying him. Mom just smiled.

Lew Hudson

A Few Quips...

Have you ever stopped to think what this old world would be like if the creator had failed to provide things to keep human beings humble. Things like mosquitoes, wood ticks, chiggers, poison ivy, houseflies, heat rash, athlete's foot, zits and all the other minor irritations of summer?

~~~~~~

Does anyone else wonder why every local television newscast in the country seems to involve a trio of good old boys or girls sitting behind a counter swapping inane small talk? Ed Murrow used to do it right on CBS. "This," he'd say, "is the news." And it was.

~~~~~~

They say students today have little appreciation for poetry which may be true. Perhaps they just aren't exposed often enough. Try this one:

> *See the kindly fisherman*
> *Wading in the creek.*
> *Hear him shout obscenities,*
> *His waders sprang a leak.*

You begin to feel the weight of your years when you go to an auction and discover items similar to your "early marriage" furnishings are now considered "early American" by young people who are willing to pay more for them than you did back when they were new.

~~~~~

Wonder why people who have lived long enough to have earned some wrinkles instruct photographers to retouch negatives so as to remove all character lines from their faces? What's wrong with a few wrinkles? Even so, most golden wedding anniversary photos give the appearance the subjects have already received final ministrations from a mortician—and who wants to be remembered that way?

~~~~~

Quick one: Which hand do you use to turn the pages of a newspaper? Well if you start reading at the front you hold the paper in your right hand and turn the first page with your left. Everyone does. But after that what happens? Do you bring your right hand over to meet the left when turning pages or do you bring your left hand over to meet the right? If you're average you do the first half of the paper by moving your left hand and the last half by moving your right. If you're doing it any other way that's probably the reason why the pages are all crooked when you get done.

...Before Closing

Readers of this column know my love of poetry. A few lines of rhyme often are the best way to express a thought. So it is, as I turn my attention toward new challenges and opportunities elsewhere, I've spent some time in my library seeking the right words with which to close out this long series of columns about "Our Corner of the Globe." I found them in a poem called "Her Letter" by one of my favorite writers, Bret Harte, who wrote:

Good-night, here's the end of my paper.
Good-night, if the longitude please.
For maybe, while wasting my taper,
Your sun's climbing over the trees.
But know, if you haven't got riches,
And are poor, dearest Joe, and all that,
That my heart's somewhere there in the ditches,
And you've struck it, on Poverty Flat.

Lew Hudson

Dispatches From Our Corner of the Globe

A Reporter Says Farewell

All I ever wanted to be was a reporter. It started when I published an underground newspaper in high school. It ends today after 43 years.

Reporters have all the fun. Reporters get to go to fires and chase police cars. Reporters get to fly with the Blue Angels. Reporters get to interview people and tell stories. Reporters get to know the leaders of business, politicians, teachers, laborers, farmers, preachers, the nerds, the nitwits, the conventional and the unconventional who make up society. Reporters are invited guests in thousands of homes every day.

Editors stay in the office and get grouchy. Reporters go to the scene and have fun. Editors make assignments. Reporters decide what to write.

It's an awesome responsibility.

Only two things are important: Is it true? Is it fair?

Reporters who concentrate on one to the exclusion of the other are unworthy of the title.

Reporters are inevitably caught up in the events they cover because they can adequately describe only that which they have experienced.

What they write affects the lives of people. Reporters can grieve with those who hurt and smile with those who rejoice but must not allow feelings to influence their writing.

In search of information, reporters listen to geniuses and buffoons, leaders and followers, the devious and the direct, the rich and the poor, the pompous and the humble.

Along the way they get to know thousands of people, each of whom is a walking, talking story waiting to be told. And if they are worth their salt, reporters come to appreciate the unique spark that burns in the soul of every human being.

That has been my goal for 30 years. To the extent I have been successful, I take pride. To the extent I have failed, I apologize.

No I am ready to retire.

The prospect both delights and frightens me. I love reporting. I love the daily give and take. I love the readers of this newspaper. At least some of them love me for which I am devoutly thankful. I have written thousands of stories, millions of words and more than 1,500 columns.

This is the last.

Thank you for your confidence. I hope I have been worthy of it. Suddenly I find myself at a loss for words, so I will borrow a few from Robert Frost, who must have felt much the same as I the day he wrote:

> *The woods are lovely, dark and deep,*
> *But I have promises to keep.*
> *And miles to go before I sleep,*
> *And miles to go before I sleep.*

--30--

Lew Hudson

We gratefully acknowledge the Brainerd Daily Dispatch and Worthington Daily Globe newspapers for allowing the use of copyrighted material for this book.

The following material originally appeared in the
Worthington Daily Globe Newspaper:

Father of the Bride; She was Dead – It Was One of Those Things; The Good Old Days?; Man on the Street; Words are Fascinating; Flexible Flyer; Long Trip Spurs Random Thoughts; Secrets of the Trade; A Rose by Any Other Name; Nightcrawler Picking Takes Talent; TV News Reporting Has Changed; A Few Quips Before Closing.

The following material originally appeared in the
Brainerd Daily Dispatch Newspaper:

Creature of Habit; In Search of a No Fault Lifestyle; A Puzzling Tale; Ever Feel Like You May be a Winner; Mr. H Doesn't Bother Reaching Out; Reporter Learns a Costly Lesson; Tune in to New Sound: Conversation; The Games We Play; Eating Apple Pie Leads to Problems; Some People Are Driven by Ambition; The Bare Truth About Lingerie; Case of the Wandering Lingerie; Battle of the Blanket; Snoring: Annoying Yet Uncontrollable; Why Do They Put Pockets in Pajamas; Zzzz...the Battle for Some Blissful Sleep; Mrs. H Controls the Rationing; Mrs. H Won't Reveal Her Secret; Top Rated Shows are Never Watched; Wallpapering Tests Marriage; Mrs. H Can Knit Up a Storm; Mrs. H Gets Her Chance to Tell All; Confessions of a Former Den Daddy; Some Baptisms Aren't So Serene; Ugly Side of the Rainbow; VW Beetle Kept Kids from Walking; Travels Without Kids: Ah the Peace and Quiet; Zip: Mrs. H Zapped Mr. H; The Father of the Bride Isn't in Spotlight; These Boots Were Made for Wearing; Uncles Can Provide Special Kind of Parenting; An Older brother's Wise Advice; The Truth Behind the Great Dogfight; Gawks Are Perfect for Squirmers; Heirloom Meets Tragic Demise; Behold Hudson's Theorem; Writer's Block is a Terrifying Dream; It's the Church that's Lost; Summer Research Work Flies By; Case of the Missing Napkin; Eating Dinner Can Be Such a Struggle Sometimes; Our Columnist Might be a Quack; Pigheaded Can Mean Big Trouble; Oh, For the Good Ol' Days (OFTGOD); Don't Mess With Breakfast of Champions; Compass Points Right Way; Christmas Comes Early for Mr. H; The Power of Negative Thinking; Fishing Wasn't a Spectator Sport for Grandpa; Baseball: an All-American Sport?; Leeches Can Be Beautiful; Fishing Outfit Belongs to Mrs. H (period); Bert Had a Way of Getting Even; A Picture Perfect Angling Adventure; One Man's Philosophy on Hunting; Tree Offers Plenty of Meaning; Some Guys Can't Be Wise Men;

Dispatches From Our Corner of the Globe

Halloween Tricks Are a Treat to Recall; A Smothered Christmas; She Wanted to Be a Christmas Star; Things Aren't Like they Used to Be; Are We All Capable of Murder?; Who Can Forget?; A Start on 'Hudson's Book of Proverbs'; Budget Restraints Should Be Taught to Lawmakers; Like Father Like Daughter; A Little Plagiarism is Just Innocent Fun; There's a Right and a Wrong Way; Harmonica Has Been a Good Friend; Classic or Popular? The Ear Knows; Tune in for the Latest Meadowlark Hit; Have You Heard 'Tingle, Tingle Brittle Car'?; Even Piccoloists Slam Oboists; Memories of a Grave Digger; Restlessness Shortens Opera Career; Zippy Little Trombone Trio; Zap! It's All in Knowing How, Dad; Due to Technical Difficulties...; Solving Bridget's Problems Doesn't Clean Slate; You Have to Show a Car Who's the Boss; A Few Easy Steps for Fixing the Car; Communicating With a Talking Post is Rough Duty; Machines Have Minds of Their Own; Outmoded Slide Rule Still Computes; Reach Out...and Touch a Computer; Case of the Balky Toaster; Why Try to Fool the Squirrels; More on the Squirrel Battle; Requiem for a Tree Frog; Animals Poised to Retaliate; Batman and Robin to the Rescue; This War With Squirrels is No New Development; Claude and Made, You Are Missed in Baxter; A Writer Says Farewell.

Lew Hudson

Dispatches From Our Corner of the Globe

ACKNOWLEDGMENTS

I thank, my ace proof reader, Jan Ann Peterson, who caught every blip and blunder I made while working on this project. You are a priceless gem. My mother, the other adept editor, also provided her expertise in finding the bloopers. Any missteps the reader finds in this book are entirely of my own making.

Thank you to my friends at the Worthington Daily Globe, Beth and Justine, who made it possible for me to trudge through the miles of dusty newspaper archives in the basement, as well as Laurie at the Nobles County Library for her kind assistance.

Sisters Cindy and LuAnn, I appreciate the infinite support and advice that you so willing provide. Thank you, LuAnn, for gathering and printing many of Dad's columns for us to enjoy. This book would not be possible without your hard work.

Dad, bless you for sharing your genes with me. It is my greatest desire to possess even a fraction of the ability that you have as a writer. Maybe one day I will.

Mom, you are a constant source of inspiration. Always there to lend support, I know you are just a phone call away when I need you. Thank you for faithfully photocopying Dad's' columns every week and mailing them to us all so that we could enjoy them.

And thank you to all who have read and enjoyed Dad's columns through the years. You are the reason that he wrote them.

Lew Hudson

Dispatches From Our Corner of the Globe

ABOUT THE AUTHORS

Lew Hudson has been a communicator all of his life. One of his earliest jobs was as a radio man at various stations across Iowa, and later at KWOA radio in Worthington, Minnesota, where he and wife Irma raised three daughters and a son. He made the transition from radio to newspaper in 1961, when he began his career as writer for the Worthington Daily Globe newspaper. Twenty years later he took a position with the Brainerd Daily Dispatch newspaper and it was there that he produced some of his most compelling writing. He is the author of, <u>From New Cloth: the Making of Worthington.</u>

Rebecca Hudson, daughter number three in the Hudson clan, has been a journalist and librarian for nearly 25 years. She has called Slayton home for most of that time and there raised two wonderful sons, Christopher and Patrick. Not having fallen far from the tree, Rebecca considers herself fortunate to have inherited many of her father's traits....and is proud of the fact that she is able to skip. Rebecca is the author and illustrator of, <u>At the Lake,</u> a memoir and collection of family recipes and reunions.

Lew Hudson